From Both Sides of the Fence

The Gifts in U

By Dee Weldon Bird

Strategic Book Group

Strategic Book Group
P.O. Box 333
Durham CT 06422
www.StrategicBookClub.com

ISBN 978-1-60976-126-4

∞

Dedication

To Ramini for being my friend and guide, and for my children Gemma, Charlotte, Leanne and Courtney for holding my hand always with no judgement, and for my Husband Kevin and my dear friend Graham, together they encouraged and believed in me as I do them. My family smile (x)

∞

CONTENTS

∞

Author's Note

Please note that I am writing about what I have personally learned about the afterlife over the years as a practicing medium. All of this information is personal to me, and I am not speaking for or on behalf of any other mediums in the world. I have used the words medium and clairvoyant in this book. These labels don't sit with me, I see myself more as a messenger. (x)

∞

ACKNOWLEDGMENTS

My life has been colorful thus far. It has been so rich, in fact, that at times it has been frowned upon and judged by others. I would like to say it has been a rainbow life—a life full of different vibrant hues thanks to all the people I have met along the way. I am so grateful to have shared so much with the folks I've encountered over the years. Through the laughs, the arguments, and even the tears of sadness, there is always joy to be found if you look hard enough.

So a big heartfelt thank you goes out to each and every one of you—for making my life experiences so full of radiance. Without you, this book would not have been possible. The journey of life is a fascinating one once the tears dry. A big smile goes out to all of you for simply being *you* and for playing your part in my journey. It does not matter if you like me or hate me, or think I'm quirky; all the labels that I am are the ingredients that make me, well, *me*.

You're all special in your own unique ways. For that, I thank you from the bottom of my heart.

And last, to the people at Eloquent/Strategic Book Publishing, for giving me a chance,

Eloquent and Strategic for me ....
Is like an extension of our family tree...
The branches shine like gold...
Sharing magic for all to see ....
Each seasons may come and go...
Strategic and Eloquent will always be seen...
Branches outstretched far and wide...
Holding the miracles born in life...
For creation written in words...
Binds the united nations of the world...
Across oceans far and wide...
The tree of strategic is alive...
A heartbeat that cannot be denied like the miracle of a new born child...
A new book born everyday a bundle of love is here to stay....
Whether written by young or old...
Strategic and Eloquent hold the key.

With SMILES and thanks and love and appreciation to you all.

Much love always
Dee(X)

∞

INTRODUCTION

Welcome to our world of universal life. This book explains life from the two sides of the fence—of the physical and spiritual realms—and then shows you how to use both sides to your advantage, rather than only using the physical body that you currently believe to be you. A forgotten truth will soon be revealed; it will give you the key back to who you really are.

This book will take you on a journey into the power of your mind and your physical body. Together, they connect and work parallel with your afterlife body. You will be able to explore and remember more of who you are. Your experiences of life on earth will open up into the bigger world in which you belong—the universal life of all life. This book connects the universal world in which we call earth with the spiritual world in which we call heaven. Soon you will learn that the two halves are, in truth, one world in which we all live together.

This book unites the two worlds we see as separate; these pages of enlightenment explain how the two worlds are not separate after all. The lives we live have many layers, facets, and frequencies. These pages will give you the tools to unlock and open you up to yourself. You will explore why you are here on earth having an earthly life experience. You will be armed with a life instructional manual, so to speak, on how to use the tools you already have inside you and to fully navigate your journey on earth. It will help explain the mysteries of death and where the deceased go. Your thoughts of life, of the earth, and of the physical being of who you are will expand. The ambiguity of life is yours to explore. It is an intricate world consisting of the physical matter and spiritual reality—a world you're not excluded from. It is a world in which you do not have to wait for until you die; you are already in the world we see as beyond. You must remember that we are already connected to everything that is—tied to all life and all of its creations. We are not separate.

The whole of the universal life is in you and around you; it always has been and always will be. It is written in truth, love, and guidance. All you need to do is take a good look in the mirror of life and see *more* than your reflection staring back.

Enjoy the exciting journey of life, and may the truth of life shine through you . . .

Much love to you,
Dee xx

∞

ONE

How it All Began

I was born to a mother and father who were both married once before. By the time they had me, they both already had grown children; having another child was the last thing on their minds.

Yes, I was an unexpected surprise. My mother's water burst on their vacation. Only then did they realize they were having another child. My mother was forty-five years old and my father was sixty-three. What a shock this must have been! My dad was in poor health and my mom was mentally ill so they already had challenges in their lives.

Life at home was hard because of my mother's illness that resulted in her being hospitalized from time to time. My dad had tuberculosis that left him in a weakened state. When I was one year old, my dad decided to put me into foster care. My mother was unable to look after me; due to her illness, she was not feeding me or caring for me very well. My dad worked so he had no other choice but to put me into foster care.

I stayed with a foster family Monday through Friday and then stayed with my parents on the weekends. This arrangement went on for about a year-and-a-half, until my dad stopped it. Between my parents and the foster family, I was getting confused about who my mother and father were. I was taken out of the foster care system to live back at home full-time with my mother and father. My dad's health got worse. He was admitted to the hospital with bronchial pneumonia from which he later died.

I was two-and-a-half years old when it became just me and my mother living at home. Luckily, the medication she was on helped a lot and she was able to look after me. My dad left my mother quite a bit of money when he passed away. Her first son wanted to borrow it to set up a café in Wales. My mother agreed to lend him the money on one condition; if anything ever happened to her, he would have to look after me. He agreed and the papers were signed.

Eleven months after my dad died, I experienced the biggest change of my life. It was the morning of December 20. I woke up as usual and went into my mother's bedroom to wake her up, too. I climbed onto her big bed—my heavy nightgown made this difficult—and crawled over her body. She was tucked under the covers, not moving.

"Mom, wake up!" I exclaimed. Nothing. *That's odd . . .* I thought.

I attempted to wake her up a few more times, kneeling beside her on the bed and holding her face in my hands. With one hand, I carefully tried to open her eyelids. Still nothing. Even at three-and-a-half years old, my instincts told me my mother was dead. I knew she was never going to wake up. Still, the innocent child in me wanted to believe otherwise. I must have cried and cried until my neighbors heard me. Alarmed, they let themselves into the house, and that's when they found me and my mother together on her bed. That morning, I had truly stared at death. It was a moment that would later become my biggest gift in life. But being a child, I just didn't know this yet.

There were many challenging years ahead of me once I became an orphan. But with inner strength and determination, those challenges helped make me the very person I am today. Over the years, I developed the gifts I have to do my readings as a medium for people.

I stayed in the country for a few months after my mother died with a few relatives I didn't know very well. Those were traumatic and abusive months. When that didn't work out, I went to stay in a children's home in Essex. I was there on and off for most of my childhood, apart from the odd foster home I would stay at in between.

The children's home I stayed in was a Catholic home run by nuns. Catholicism was a religion that I found, in parts, interesting—such as having ash on my forehead on Ash Wednesday. I also enjoyed holding the lovely beads on the rosary. The rosary fascinated me because each bead had a different meaning.

It was during this time that I started to notice I was different from other kids. I was seven years old. I would often say to my friends, "Hey, can you see that person over there?" They would always tell me no. I thought it was odd that they couldn't see who, or what, I saw; it all felt so normal and easy to me. In fact, I had always just assumed that everyone could see the same things. I started wondering if perhaps I had been given a gift because both of my parents had died. It wasn't until my friends laughed and starting suggesting that I was a bit odd that I soon stopped talking about seeing *others*. I decided it would be best to keep my secret to myself.

I tried to block out my sixth sense all during my childhood. Honestly, seeing dead people when I was a kid never really scared me the way one would think it should. It was all of the gossip from other people that actually put fear into me and make me question if

I was "normal" or not. At twelve years old, I became very confused.

I was taken in by a vicar and his family. Being Christians, they considered my experiences "evil." As much as I wanted to keep these sightings to myself, I couldn't. When I turned fourteen years old, I began seeing dead people, or ghosts, every night when I was in bed. I would just lie there, not understanding why this was happening to *me*. What did they want with me? My foster family sent me for tests at the hospital—sleep tests and brain scans in case I was mentally ill like my mother had been. My foster family and the various doctors and specialists I saw couldn't understand or explain why I was seeing what I was seeing. After my hospital test results came back, I was told I had epilepsy. Even though I had never had any fits, I was prescribed tablets for my condition.

I took the medication for a few weeks but it made me so ill that I simply stopped taking it altogether. Strangely, I was never asked to go back to the hospital for an update, and my foster family never mentioned the tablets again. Again, I told myself that I needed to keep the entire thing a secret. I started going to bed each night with the light on. I had many different experiences during these nights—things I couldn't explain to anyone. I could see things I knew no one else could see. No one would believe me if I attempted to share my visions. They wouldn't believe me; they'd think I was crazy. It became, at times, a very lonely, isolated world.

Much more activity started happening when I entered my twenties. My work pens would randomly disappear and reappear. I would sometimes suddenly see smoke rings in the air—when no one was smoking. Spirit people would walk down my garden path at my house. Murder victims would come to see me. I found myself shaking hands with a relative who had passed a few years before; her hand was so lovely and warm to the touch that my hand stayed hot the rest of that day. These were just a few of the encounters back then. I started to take these experiences seriously. Obviously, I was somehow chosen to have this gift. I started forming questions in my mind: *How would I use this gift to help others? Would they even believe me?* We live in a pretty skeptical world.

To do a reading, I would say 5 percent is based on what is here in the present, and the other 95 percent is in the understanding of what goes on behind the scenes. My work is my passion; I do it from my heart and soul, with love and guidance, and, in truth, to the best of my ability. Looking back, I called this my little love balloon; although you can't see it, it doesn't mean it's not there. It kept me alive and helped me through some pretty tough times growing up. I truly believe that all of the support, guidance, and love that kept my love balloon in the air was a gift my mother had passed down to me after she died. At times, it was all I had, and yet it was all I needed to survive.

RAMINI

I focused my energy on developing my craft. At the same time, I began forming a strong relationship with my spirit guide, Ramini. Ramini and I have been communicating since birth—and even before that. We shared a previous life experience together as brother and sister.

Let me explain. Back in my late twenties and early thirties, I was asked to join a group where people developed their mediumship with the help of a teacher. Admittedly, I was a bit naïve about spiritual organizations. (I had grown up with my gift; it was natural to me, like breathing.) And as I began attending the sessions, I found myself in some pretty interesting situations with the other participants in the circle. At the end of the sessions, however, I realized it was all collective in my learning. My gift was developing rapidly during each class; I was able to get a better grasp on the concept that everything in life has value and meaning.

One day, the teacher asked us to figure out the names of our guides. She wanted us to find out a little about them, too, and then share the information with the class. I left the circle feeling confused and dumbfounded. Questions began flooding my mind: *How do I do that? What if he doesn't tell me his name?* (I always felt that my guide was a he, so at least that was a start.) *What if my imagination begins playing tricks on me?*

I had some free time that weekend and decided it was the perfect opportunity to try and talk with my guide. *Let's find out who you really are*, I thought, grabbing a pad of paper and a pen. I sat down at the table and cleared my mind. Then I began focusing all of my thoughts and energy on my guide.

The name appeared first. After a few moments of concentration, I was shown different letters—almost like someone was holding flashcards up in front of me—and I scribbled them down. *R . . . A . . .* M *. . . I . . .* N *. . . I . . .* I said in my mind. I moved my head a few inches away from the paper. "Ramini," I whispered.

Is that right? I wondered. My heart began to pick up its pace. *I can't make this up*, I thought anxiously. *I mean, where would that come from? I have never heard a name 'Ramini' before in my life*. Deep down, I knew I was right. Ramini had confirmed what I had written down. I smiled, pleased to have a name to connect with my guide. I took a deep breath and let it out slowly.

Next, I had to try and associate a face with Ramini's name. I focused on space in the air around me and asked him to show himself. Sure enough, he did. At first, he appeared very close to my face, so close that he was out of focus. But he slowly moved away, as if I was using the zoom-out feature of a digital camera, and I could see him more clearly. *Thank you*, I thought.

He looked like a North American Indian. He had long black shoulder-length hair and a slim build. His eyes seemed kind and approachable; his face didn't intimidate me at all. He gazed back at me with an all-knowing expression. In fact, he *did* know almost everything about me. I mean, he had been my guide for years! To see him standing in front of me felt so natural; it was a very heartwarming moment. I stared at him, partly in awe and partly to familiarize myself with him and his essence and vibration.

Time stood still. And when I had memorized everything about him, I smiled and thanked him for showing up. More importantly, I thanked him for guiding me ever since I was a lost and confused child. He smiled back and nodded. When he disappeared, I chuckled to myself. I was so happy to be able to go back to the circle the following week and share my first visual experience with Ramini with them. I wasn't sure how my teacher or the other participants would react, but one thing was for sure: My relationship with Ramini grew even more that day.

Ramini's character is very multi-faceted, to say the least. There are no real words I can use to accurately sum him up. He is often childlike and funny. These characteristics make it hard for me to be cross with him for very long. He reminds me of things I need to do when I forget (like when the electric meter is running out). He always looks out for me, protecting me from danger. He is very knowledgeable and teaches me lessons about how he used to live, using all parts of a dead animal for medicine, clothing, and survival—a lesson that lasted two hours. He constantly makes me laugh.

On one occasion, Ramini and I were working together on a missing person case. It was an intense case for me because I didn't really know what I was doing at the time. Basically, I was thrown into the deep end and had to figure everything out on my own.

Looking back, I think it was a test of my morals and values and how strong I am in this line of work.

One day, I was feeling frustrated and angry. Suddenly, Ramini showed me a volcano. *What does this have to do with anything?* I demanded in my head. Aggravated, I ranted about how I didn't have time to play games. I needed to focus on work and be serious. Unaffected by my attitude, Ramini replied, *It's* you! *You are like a volcano!* I couldn't help but laugh at what he was comparing me to. His sense of humor has always had a way of calming me down.

As I continued to go to the medium workshops, I must confess that I cheated a bit with the help of Ramini. On one occasion, we were learning about chakras. The teacher began asking us questions about the various colors they can be. At one point, she wanted us to tell her what color hers was. Everyone called out different colors, but no one could answer correctly. Finally, I called out what color I thought her chakra was and got it right! The teacher praised me for this, but I had actually been told the answer by Ramini. He knew I was not confident in classrooms and decided to help me out.

I smiled inwardly and realized that no matter what situation I found myself in, I'd always have guidance and support from Ramini when I needed it. The connections I have with him and my other spirit friends are incredibly strong, especially the ones that began when I was growing up.

While I am grateful for the time I spent in the circle workshops, in the end they weren't for me. They helped me build up my confidence and practice my craft as a medium. They also gave me the chance to expand upon my gift and challenge my mind. The best thing I took away from them, however, was the fact that I now had an even better connection with Ramini.

It has taken almost all of my life to realize that I was given this special gift for a reason. I couldn't have figured it out without the help of my guides; they have taught me well. They have been supportive and understanding of everything. But I also couldn't have become at peace with this if it wasn't for my loving children and closest friends. All of these people and spirits have become my inner circle. They have helped me adjust to this unique way of life.

∞

TWO

A Guided Tour Around The Afterlife (You Don't Die)

I want to clear up the mystery of what seems so final: *death*. First of all, we don't die; there is no such thing. We are more *dead* living our experiences here on earth than we ever will be when we die—or, more accurately said, when we let go of our physical bodies. Only when we truly let go do we become more alive.

After many years of doing various types of readings for all sorts of people, I was given an insight into a secret world—one which seems to only be accessible by spirits and mediums. But this never sat well with me; we are *all* from the afterlife. In fact, everyone just visits here, if you will, to have a life experience. And we become so engrossed in what is going on around us when we are visiting here that we forget where we came from.

You see, living here on earth gives us a different frequency and energy vibration from what we give off in the afterlife. As I mentioned, we forget the whole picture of who we are, why we are here, and where we came from. We must work out our earthly experiences while we are here in our limited awake feelings. Unfortunately, we often get distracted with outside matter.

Most people who seek out readings are folks who desperately want some kind of proof of life after death. They want readings as a type of validation from their loved ones who have passed on. They want to know more about the afterlife. They are interested in what their loved ones are doing. It is my job to ask these everyday questions. I am the bridge between the living and the dead.

And this is what this guided tour is all about. As I take you on this fascinating journey, I will try to keep it as simple as possible; I do not want words to make the whole experience complicated. At the end of this journey, hopefully you will realize how fun, alive, loving, and caring the afterlife really is. All of your fears and uncertainty will be dispelled.

The fear factor associated with death needs to be destroyed. There is an illusion that dead people are something to be afraid of. Why, I ask you? I can bet that a large part of it has to do with the fear of the unknown. Furthermore, when people lack knowledge, truth, and understanding, they have hesitations; their imaginations can get the best of them. Anyone can make up stories about the afterlife, and no one will know if he or she is being truthful. We have limited proof available to us, and even that can be questionable.

But there's hope. The mediums who actually work in truth are not tarnished with all the labels associated with mediumship. Remember, I am not here to change people's views or opinions; I am just sharing my truth. You can make up your own minds on what feels right to you after all is said and done, and what you want to believe...enough of me waffling...

WELCOME TO THE AFTERLIFE TOUR

Were you thinking you would have to splurge on airfare? Nope, you don't have to travel! Once we leave the physical earth, we are already in the afterlife. You see, we never really left. Earthly experiences are an extension of the afterlife, kind of like if you build an extension to your home. Just because you have forgotten and can't see the afterlife doesn't mean it's not around us.

We have physical bodies on earth; in the afterlife we don't. We also have different energy vibrations and frequencies on earth compared to in the afterlife. Try to liken the different energy vibrations to suddenly using a different language. For example, there are thousands of different languages used by different countries in the world. We may never hear or become aware of them in our lifetimes, yet we accept and trust they are out there.

Our lives on earth mirror the truth and answers of the afterlife in a shadow form, similar to walking down the street and seeing your shadow on the pavement. That outline of your body—that shadow—represents the *physical* body. Your *real* body is the one you will see in the afterlife when you move on.

We can all agree that we have physical bodies; it is easy to agree upon this because we can see them and use them on a daily basis. Our bodies are different and unique to us and assist us in our earthly experiences. But our physical bodies are not us—the real us, that is. Instead, they are our personal vehicles, per se. When we have had enough exploring and experiencing life on earth with them, we discard them and step out of them, much like getting out of our cars each day. Our bodies, as well as all the things we use on earth, are the tools that aid us in our life experiences. Our body vehicles are perfect for earth. If they weren't, we would probably have been born with astronaut suits on!

So what happens when we step out of our physical bodies for good? For starters, you get to choose what you want to look like for the afterlife. You have a lot more choices in how you want to express and show yourself—the *real* you. With our physical bodies, our options are limited—unless we want to pay for expensive plastic surgery. None of this is needed in the afterlife. (However, if you still want to live in such a way as you did on earth with all its limitations, you can.) Whether you're having your experiences here on earth or in the afterlife, the same rule still applies: free will and choice! Remember, that always belongs to you.

Our afterlife bodies don't experience illness or deformities of any kind. Our new bodies are made of strong energy and vibrations. They are free with a freedom that is not ruled like the physical body in how it looks or doesn't look. There is never any need to hide or be self-conscious. The afterlife body is an all-emanating, multi-faceted body that can do so much more than the physical body can. For a simple visual picture, imagine your physical body as a peddle car. Your afterlife body would then be a multi-functioning, sleek and stylish sports car—the greatest model of all time.

You now know the differences between our real bodies and our earthly bodies. Both versions stay together throughout our earthly journey; they are never separated or detached from each other. Some folks refer to the energy around our physical bodies as an "aura."

But how do I know all of this? How am I so sure that our spirit bodies are our *real* bodies and our physical bodies are just vehicles, or tools, to get us through our earthly experiences? Let me share a personal anecdote with you. It happened just a few years ago.

I had been living with a close friend for a number of years. One night, we went to bed, as usual. After we had fallen asleep, I suddenly woke up to the sounds of my friend calling out my name.

I sat up in bed and noticed my friend standing in the bedroom doorway. *What the heck?* I thought. I could hear my friend snoring; I looked down at my side to see my friend fast asleep with their pajamas on. Yet, my friend was also standing in the doorway with all outdoor clothes on. They were holding up a garment of mine and asking me questions about it. Completely confused, I kept looking at my friend in different clothes in the doorway and then back to my same friend in bed fast asleep next to me.

How is this possible to be able to see two of my same friend at the same time in the same room—one asleep and one awake? I wondered. I was especially perplexed because my friend had not died yet. Had that been the case, I would've been more at ease about the situation. After all, I was used to seeing spirit people. But this was a living person on our side of the fence!

After a period of time (and not much sleep after that), I realized what the experience was teaching me about the afterlife: *You do not have to wait until you die before you get your real body/afterlife body.* You already have it. Your real body is yours for all eternity. It turns out that my friend's real body awoke that night to visit everyone in the afterlife; mediums call this a "dream experience." Physically, we may forget our connections and our real homes, but our real bodies and souls never do. This is so that when we leave our physical vehicle bodies and suddenly remember who we really are, our conscious thoughts and understanding of what we want to believe becomes clear. We don't go into mental or spiritual shock.

Every night, we all visit the afterlife in one way or another without any harm or fear. Our lack of remembering is what confuses the vibrations between the afterlife and our earthly lives. This is why our dreams can seem so vivid and real—and sometimes scary. It all depends on our fears, thoughts, and feelings, and how entangled the frequency has become from one vibration to the other. Simply put, think of the afterlife frequency as a radio station. Our earthly frequency is another one. When going from one to the other, we hear a bit of both stations and maybe a little static until we fully switch over. At night, both frequencies sometimes mix together and resonate in your dream experiences. This happens *every* night, yet we don't realize this. We also hardly ever remember our dreams.

∞

THREE

Guided Afterlife Tour—Communication On Both Sides

There is always communication going on between our real bodies and our physical bodies. We have thoughts and we have speech, or words, but they are both forms of communication; they're just expressed in different ways.

Our Physical Bodies

We are all aware of the five human senses: seeing, listening, smelling, tasting, and touching. And we are lucky enough to have so many options in how we choose to communicate with each other on earth. The most used ways of communicating are through talking and listening. But we sometimes take this for granted when we mix communicating with each other with our busy and distracting lifestyles. We often find ourselves on autopilot. We take turns talking and listening but we're not *really* talking and listening.

Lack of focus can cause miscommunication and confusion for all parties involved. I often refer to this as crossing wires.

The language we use as we correspond with one another can, at times, be very limiting. It can also be interpreted in many different ways. I'm sure many of you have experienced this from time to time. You try to explain something your way and it is interpreted another way by the other person. This can cause a lot of confusion, especially because people are often afraid to speak the truth. They tend to lean toward saying what people *want* to hear rather than saying how they really *feel*.

Basically, we live in a world that is an illusion. We do not share who we really are, what we are about, or how we really feel. We become part of an illusion trap, if you will, to fit in. Doing so leaves us all in a tangled mess. Our words, thoughts, and shared feelings do not make any sense. We end up arguing, fighting, and desperately trying to be understood. Exasperating, isn't it?

We use up our energy by communicating within the boundaries of not speaking our true thoughts and feelings; we are so used to feeling like it is okay to lie to ourselves and to others. We deny ourselves free speech within free will and choice. We think, *It's okay to lie to make so-and-so happy* and *It's okay to lie and not share all of my feelings toward someone*. We opt on sharing only fragments of ourselves, letting others try to piece together the jigsaw puzzle of communication so what we're saying makes sense—so *we* make sense.

Communication is easy if all the barriers and limitations and expectations and, most importantly, *fear* that we put in the way are removed. Communication would be much easier if only we could learn to trust our feelings from the heart rather than be skeptical by the words of the mind. We would have far less fighting going on between all of us. Perhaps we would actually get to know each other and understand one another.

Saying what we actually really mean would be a good place to start. I found out at a very young age that people don't like the truth. They only like the illusion, which is somewhat of a comfort blanket—a lie that we can conveniently hide behind. We often feel naked when we attempt to be open and honest because we are so used to covering up. But we need to remember to share, talk, and communicate in ways that actually benefit not only ourselves but the people we surround ourselves with. While we may not always like what we hear, we should appreciate when words come from the heart in truth. Deep down, we often know the difference between right and wrong; we just don't always want to admit it. This could be because of many reasons, including pride, ego, etc.

I think you get my drift: Be honest as you communicate. Speak from the heart. Truth is always for our own good, especially when it comes to love. But what should we do if, for some reason, we cannot speak at all? What if we can't see or hear? Well, our other senses begin to overcompensate for the missing ones. For example, if someone is deaf, that person will rely on his or her sight to communicate through body language and senses of instincts and feeling. If someone is blind, he or she will tune into their ability to touch in order to feel and sense things. You see, we all have backup plans when it comes to communication.

So those are the basic guidelines of how our physical bodies are used to communicate. Now I will explain how the afterlife spirits use their bodies to communicate. You will also begin to understand why you have your afterlife body with you now and for all eternity.

As I just mentioned, our physical bodies' senses overcompensate for any senses that may not work properly. Well, our physical bodies use our eternal bodies, or our afterlife bodies, as backups, too. Both bodies co-exist while we have our life experiences on earth. Our afterlife bodies guide us—almost as if we have built-in navigational systems—and help us navigate our crazy world. Unfortunately, we are not taught that we all have afterlife bodies that stay with our physical bodies. We only find out after we have let go of our physical bodies when they are no longer needed. Soon, you will see why letting go of our earthly bodies when our time has come is a joyous celebration.

You're probably thinking, *How is death a celebration?* Well, the sadness we feel over the death of a loved one is actually for ourselves. Our souls know the truth that those who have let go have gone back home to an amazing place. (Imagine the best vacation destination ever.)

Earth is like a giant school of learning. The funny thing is, however, is that most of us hate school as children. But when we have more experiences under our belts, we begin to feel differently about it. How many times have you heard adults say, "Oh, if I could go back to school again, I would do things differently . . ."? Or have you ever heard someone say, "If only I knew then what I know now . . ."? Sound familiar? This is exactly what we are doing when we come from the afterlife to "go to school" as earthly beings.

A lot of what we say and do mirrors the afterlife truth in a "shadow way," meaning we are able to understand as much as we want to understand. This also occurs so that our afterlife bodies do not get in the way of our free will and choice in the experiences we choose to participate in while on earth. Perhaps you've encountered a strange coincidence before. Or maybe you thought fate or intuition played a key factor in something you decided to do. Or have you ever experienced a bout of déjà vu? These interesting moments are all part of us interacting with our afterlife bodies on a subconscious level.

The little internal voice I talk about—the other half of you—is your friend. Embrace this side. Embracing the other half, your spiritual afterlife half, is part of a process called tuning into your 'other' sense, or your sixth sense. Ever see the movie, *The Sixth Sense*, starring Bruce Willis? The sixth sense is a vibration and energy that is communicated by thought or feeling. It is a sense that that flows through you and around you; it is not consumed and dormant in your head. We may think that we're carrying on in our everyday lives, but are you getting the sense that there is a lot more going on behind the scenes than we think?

These hunches . . . gut instincts . . . intuition—whatever you want to call it—is you using your afterlife body. Chances are, you probably didn't even know this is what you were doing! During these times, you are connecting to your truth and your real you. The moment was probably unbelievably quick, but it had a huge impact on you and got your total attention because these kinds of experiences don't happen on a regular basis. These moments feel different to the physical body; we suddenly feel free from all the limitations and barriers that we face within our physical bodies. (You would like more of this, right?)

We think these higher truths and feelings are out of reach because we are merely physical bodies. We assume these new powers will only become available to us when we are dead or if we communicate with mediums. I'm here to tell you that you have amazing possibilities within yourself. All you need to do is focus on the two bodies that you have—your physical body *and* your afterlife body. The best part is that you can start opening your eyes to what is around you right now.

You can tune into it more by opening yourself up and by practicing listening out for your own navigational system within you—that little voice that talks to you from time to time. That voice is your afterlife body talking to your physical body. Remember, as with anything you do, the more you practice, the more natural it feels.

When I am given messages from the afterlife, I receive them as thoughts. Plus, I am able to mentally see them. It is similar to watching a mini film, or reading cue cards. I rely more on visual cues as I prefer to receive lots of detail, but that is not always possible. I have heard voices from time to time, too. But these voices are not like regular voices we use in our everyday conversations. Those sound waves enter our ears from outside; afterlife voices come from within the ear.

Afterlife spirits use whatever sense is better for their recipients to receive their messages with. It all depends on what senses are predominantly used by the person on earth. However, thought seems to be the main form of communication used (unless by their own free will and choice they prefer to communicate like they did on earth). Again, it's all down to personal choice. However, once afterlife spirits who don't typically use thought communication realize how instant and easy it actually is, they usually switch to it.

As soon as an afterlife spirit thinks a thought, it is received by the medium instantly. With our physical bodies, we have a time delay because talking and thinking are so much slower and more difficult to do and process. For example, you call someone on the telephone and say, "Hello, is so-and-so there, please?" Then there is a delay or pause because you must wait for an answer. At the same time, this gap gives us time to think and worry within our thoughts. While we're waiting for an answer (or for the person who answers the phone to go get the person we've asked for), our minds can run wild: *I hope it is okay to call at this hour. Will he/she be cross with me? Will he/she be too busy to come to the phone?* All of the little conversations that we have with ourselves can make us worry and stress out over nothing in our everyday lives. We sometimes talk ourselves into things and create imaginary negative situations that have not happened or won't even happen.

This is the power of fear. This is the brain talking and replaying learned behavior patterns. When we assume thoughts, we make life much more difficult for ourselves. But it doesn't have to be that way. If only we just waited for the answer and accepted the few seconds of silence for what it truly was—silence—then we would use much less energy on a daily basis. No wonder we have headaches and worry so much! Our thoughts can make us behave in self-destructing behaviors without even realizing it.

It always comes back to the self—self-responsibility and self-ownership of our thoughts. It is no wonder why the afterlife people choose instant thought from their hearts as their primary means of communication; it is quick and saves a lot of time and confusion! The reason why we have difficulty understanding this concept is because we are used to relying on talking and listening quickly. We do not have time to *really* listen to our afterlife body thoughts. In fact, we forget our afterlife bodies are even there unless they randomly get our attention through a hunch, instinct, or déjà vu moment.

Yes, instant thought can be tricky to wrap your head around; it definitely was for me at first. But give it a chance. Once you see the benefits of thought communication and how much easier it makes life, we begin to understand so much more about ourselves and each other. Understanding is the key to peace and acceptance, and that's also where love grows.

Remember, communication can occur in many different forms. Use it to your advantage and embrace it. Don't treat it like your enemy, and please don't create unnecessary stress with worrying about communication that hasn't even taken place. In the end, it all boils down to our own individual attitudes and what we experience when we truly open up our hearts and our minds.

∞

FOUR

Out of Control, Out of My Mind

The mind is a lot like gears on a car. Specifically, the mind is a lot like gears on a sports car. It's all about the *speed*. Our thoughts travel at such a fast speed that they pop up before we even know it. Have you ever accidentally blurted something out by accident and then wished you hadn't said it? Blame your brain; it's like it has control of itself, almost as if on autopilot.

There have been times when I have been really busy, focusing on a task that takes up all of my attention. Suddenly, my youngest child will attempt to strike up a conversation with me. I'll be vaguely aware of what she's saying, all the while still trying to concentrate on what I am doing. I'll give the right replies, or so I think, and silently praise myself for my ability to multitask so easily. But the next day when I have free time, my youngest will remind me about our conversation the day before. Sadly, I'll hardly have any idea what she's talking about, knowing full well I had not given her my full attention during our exchange of words.

I *should* have been truthful and told her that I had not been giving her my full attention at the time. I had been in my own moment, not hers. This is what I call being in the "same book but on a different page" as someone else. Sometimes, we may just be on different paragraphs of the same page, trying to bridge the gap of one experience into another.

FIGHTING THOUGHTS AND THE ECHO OF THOUGHTS . . .

Thoughts are like being in a big hallway. Thoughts travel a lot like sounds do. Have you ever been in a two-way conversation where your thoughts are actually being said during your exchange of words? Think about it. It gives a whole new meaning to the phrase "two-way conversation"! When that occurs, an echo of thoughts in your mind parallel your words. Here's an example:

You say, "I *did* take out the trash!"

Your significant other replies, "No, you didn't!"

After you insist that you did take out the trash, the next split second gap of waiting for your significant other's reply enables you to begin having a conversation of thoughts in your head. While you are told that you didn't take out the trash, you say in your head, *Yes, I did. I remember walking out of the kitchen to the garden and getting the trash bin from the shed!*

After a lengthy debate, your significant other finally says, "Okay, well, I found one bag of trash tucked behind the lawnmower . . ." In your mind, you may say, *At least the bin was taken out to the curb! See? I did take the trash out!* Instead, you reply, "Oh, I'm sorry I didn't see that bag. Thank you for getting it for me."

Technically, both people are right. What they are arguing about in thought form is just the missing detail of one bag that was not put out. This dominates the whole conversation of the wrong meaning in the first place. If your significant other had said, "You know when you put the trash out today? Well, you missed one bag. I found it tucked behind the lawnmower!" This would have changed the whole conversation from a battle of thought to a flowing conversation of facts.

You can see how facts play a vital role in how conversations of thoughts are reflected and received. They have the ability to govern how the rest of the thought process can unfold. The facts and the echo of our own thoughts during a conversation are like two of us taking part in a conversation with others; it can get confusing quickly! However, when we make a conscious effort to slow down, we learn to really *listen* to thoughts. When we really listen, we can then observe, work out what the thoughts mean, and then reply with a more accurate response.

Your two bodies—your physical body and your afterlife body—often have thoughts at the same time, but both bodies have different thought patterns. We notice these different thought patterns more when we are by ourselves. For example, say we decide to start a new diet that dictates what food groups we shall eat. Usually, we cut out the sweets, right? The diet starts off really well, and so far we've had three days of "being good." But on day four, we open the kitchen cupboards to see a package of chocolate chip cookies staring right back at us.

Your afterlife body thinks, *Oh, look at those yummy chocolate chip cookies!* Your physical body thinks, *I have been so good for three days. No, I will not stray off my diet.* And even though we should probably walk away, we don't. Our thoughts continue. *Oh, let me just hold the package and take a look . . .* We may even ask other people if they want some cookies. Of course, they decline the offer. Meanwhile, we wish they had said yes. That way, we'd be able to justify indulging just this once . . .

We may spend all day having thoughts about those darn cookies. Our afterlife and physical thoughts participate in a tug-of-war; one thought pattern is all for us having a cookie, while the other half is very against the idea! Whichever one wins the battle depends on our moods, thoughts, and feelings at the time. If we feel good about ourselves, we may find more reasons to say no. Yet, if we feel vulnerable or not very self-confident, we are more likely to say yes and give in to having a cookie or two . . . or six. Remember that our thoughts govern our actions.

Most arguments happen because we are not listening to the other person who is talking to us during a conversation. Instead, we tend to listen to ourselves. We focus on our own thoughts—bartering, arguing, threatening, forcing. We focus on using the communication tools and techniques to win our thought battles from within.

Why does there always have to be a winner and a loser with everything we do? Why can't we call a truce? Can we at least agree to disagree? Sadly, we live in a busy, fast-paced world. We are so accustomed to *do* and not think—or at least think *after* the fact—that our intended messages can easily become skewed. Furthermore, we sometimes make choices and decisions at the cost of others because the patience of true communication process is not applied.

Thoughts have many echoes of other thoughts. We are always participating in internal and external conversations—and often at the same time. These internal and external conversations make it easy for us to talk ourselves into or out of actions we take next. Our thoughts can also run away with us, too. Thoughts of fear, conclusions, expectations, etc., can become overwhelming. Suddenly, we feel like we are losing our minds. Our thoughts have the ability to easily get all tangled up in a mess of cross wires. To get out of these predicaments, we need to remember to think and communicate clearly with ourselves and with others the first time around.

SINGLING OUT OUR SILENT THOUGHTS

We know that spoken thoughts are very selective. We select what facts and what meanings we share with others. We tend to divulge only parts of the whole, carefully selecting our words in our everyday conversations. Because we only communicate with bits and pieces of our thoughts, however, it's easy to see why life often seems like such a puzzle.

Let me try to explain further. Take, for example, the unfortunate deadly accident in February 2010 involving a SeaWorld trainer named Dawn Brancheau and an orca whale. Media outlets all over the world covered the incident. Most headlines read something along the lines of: WHALE KILLS TRAINER AT SEAWORLD IN FLORIDA. Anyone glancing at the headline would probably think, *A whale killed an innocent human being.*

It does not matter if an action is made by a human, an animal, or even a marine mammal in this case. (Yes, animals have thoughts, feelings, and senses, too.) We *all* share similar thoughts. The only thing that separates us is how our thoughts are expressed. Humans use speech, body language, and sign language to share thoughts and interact with each other; animals use their own sounds and body language. It's not an animal's fault if we do not understand the language of thought in which it is trying to communicate. It is also not a human's fault. We must remember that misunderstandings occur all the time.

With that said, if the orca whale that killed the SeaWorld trainer actually intended to kill her, it would have done so a long time ago. We need to always communicate with caution—especially around animals living in captivity.

Imagine SeaWorld as an acting school for whales. The top performers of the class get to perform all sorts of tricks for the paying public. These whales stay on their best behavior. Yet the whales that are poor performers, or those that are temperamental and need more work, have to stay in the smaller tanks. They don't receive as much praise or treats as the good whales. They also don't get to experience the bits of freedom the good whales get. No one likes to be left out for long. In fact, when we do feel left out, our attention soon turns elsewhere because we do not feel as important as the others who are included in whatever is going on.

The good whales get to do fun tricks. The audience claps excitedly and the trainers praise the whales for being so clever. But for the other whales, boredom and frustration eventually set in. They long to be like the performing whales—to be given a chance to act for the public and get lots of praise, too. Tillikum, the whale in the accident, had been singled out. He did not understand why he was being treated differently from other whales. After all, they are all the same creatures—even to look at—right?

This one particular day in February, Tillikum had had enough of being left out of the performances. He wanted to join in on all the fun, too. Not realizing he had not been trained on how to communicate properly with humans, he behaved the only way he knew how to: like an orca whale.

The big show finished up just like any other whale show at SeaWorld. The trainer showed the audience how she massaged the whales' bellies. The audience clapped while the trainer praised Tillikum. He rolled over, loving all of the attention. Suddenly, it was time for the trainer to walk away. Tillikum didn't understand why. He wanted to play more! In fact, he wanted to get the trainer in the water. With a little effort, Tillikum raised his massive body out of the pool and grabbed the trainer, pulling her into the water. All he wanted to do was play—to do tricks like she would do with the other whales!

He became confused when the trainer was not playing. Why was she staying under the water and not swimming with him? *Why?* Perplexed ,the whale began to thrash about with her. He thought he was playing with her, all the while underestimating his own strength. He didn't realize how fragile humans are; he hadn't been properly trained. The trainer died in the accident. Who should be held responsible for her untimely death? The orca whale? The trainer? SeaWorld? To this day, it remains a controversial question.

Whales are social creatures that play a lot. In fact, whales (and dolphins) are incredibly clever. They can sense danger when it is present. They have even helped humans when they have been in trouble at sea. Furthermore, they know and sense when someone is ill with a disease. But if they are this smart, shouldn't we be designating as much time to understanding their thoughts and feelings as we do with training them to perform?

Whales are big moneymakers in water theme parks. Some argue that these places are safe havens for them—conservation centers. They say that the whales are happy where they are. They have food readily available. They don't have to fight for survival in captivity. Okay, fine. So if I capture you and put you in a big metal box, opening the lid every now and then so that you can perform tricks for me, would you be happy? Don't worry. I'd give you plenty of food, too, for doing the tricks. Heck, you won't have to work a real job ever again! I'd give you everything you need . . . Would you be happy?

Try imagining your freedom and natural habitat being taken away from you. Imagine being put into a metal box similar to a house, but much smaller. You would want your natural home back. Something inside of you would be telling you that something is not right with your situation. This feeling is inherent. As a child, I had never been taught what death was or what it looked like. Yet, when

I found my mother dead in her room, something inside me *knew* what it was. This is instinct. Humans have it and so do all animals. Just because some animals are born into captivity, their instincts still tell them that they are not in their natural homes. Wild animals are wild for a reason.

Did the orca whale kill like all of the headlines seemed to suggest? Or was he just trying to share his thoughts? Did he simply want to play a little longer? I will let you make up your own mind on this, but I feel through sense and instinct that these mammals have feelings and thoughts, just like we do. We don't listen to them because our own thoughts are too busy elsewhere, or we just focus on what we want to see—the sensationalized version of everything. All too often actions get noticed without anyone looking at the meaning of *why?* There is always a reason why behind every action, which is determined by thought, if we spend the time finding out what it is.

I have seen how children who are misunderstood are singled out and labeled as naughty when they act up. They are told to sit at their desks in the corner of a classroom . . . or face a wall . . . or go to their bedrooms. They are told that they are bad and do not get to participate in what the "good" people in the family, class, or particular group are doing. Why does it have to be this way? Is it because we do not understand someone, or know how to handle them, and therefore banish them away? It's similar to how the orca whales are treated. Is this the only way humans know how to behave? Obviously, it doesn't work. All it does is cause more of what is already going on—more thoughts of rejection. Isolation of thoughts has the ability to cause more harm than good. That much is certain.

The same type of thing happened to my daughter at school. She had been punished for something she didn't do, and she had to miss a week of recess. Well, she was being bullied by another classmate at the time. Her punishment meant she could not mix with her friends, which caused more harm and suffering than if the school had actually listened to her thoughts in the first place rather than jumping to conclusions and enforcing a punishment for something she had not done. Sadly, this tends to be our thought communication process. We act before communicating. We don't try to understand all sides to a story. And if we communicate (for lack of a better word) this way in human-to-human interaction, what chance do animals or mammals have when communicating with us? Furthermore, we wonder why we fight for justice. We would not have to if we actually learned how to listen and communicate effectively.

Keep hold of your steering wheel of thoughts—keep control of the gears—and remember to signal, or communicate properly, when moving on. Thoughts are an art if you think about it. Simply put, if learned, we understand. Fully enjoy other people's thoughts as much as your own. At the same time, remember that in thought we are never alone. Wildlife and domestic animals have thoughts and communicate, too; the gift belongs to *all* of us.

∞

FIVE

LOVE IS EVERYTHING

Every experience humankind has ever had has been about discovering the truth and remembering the eternal meaning of love. Simply put, love is *everything*. While this is the truth, it may be difficult to understand the concept because of the many different love experiences we have had. If you think about it, love can be found in every encounter we have ever had—whether it is the lessons in love that we give to others, or the lessons in love that we receive. In the end, it is all still love . . .

If we allow ourselves to go deeper beyond the surface of the material world that shadows and hides the amazing truth, love will emanate no matter what situation we may find ourselves in. It will always be the main driving force behind everything we do. The only thing that shadows love is fear. In fact, it clouds the vibration of love. If we open up our hearts and minds to the whole picture of each of our experiences, we can better understand the meaning of love.

All we have to do is remember a subtle truth: With every experience we have, it will have two halves. This splitting action, so to speak, enables us to see an experience in a multi-faceted way—with many outcomes, reasons, and meanings exposed. We are able to learn from the experience, accept the outcome, forgive (if applicable), and acknowledge the experience as a whole. (The only way our viewpoints would become clouded is if one emotion suddenly takes over and we become blinded to the true lessons being learned).

The truth offers back to us our ability to see and feel our own love from within. We need to harness our energy and focus on ourselves just as much as we focus on others around us. If we can achieve that balance, we will then learn to fully understand what an experience is trying to teach us. Unfortunately, we tend to only experience what we need or what we can mentally cope with. At the same time, our various experiences help us to continually grow mentally and physically. With practice, we have the ability to get in tune with our higher selves. We can clearly listen to our little voices of reason.

It is important to remember that while *we*, as humankind, are part of everything, we are primarily responsible for *ourselves* and our own actions. Our actions always cause chain reaction effects. Have you ever heard the saying, "You reap what you sow"? It is basically about your own free will and choice.

Again, the instructions of life consist of one simple step: love. It is a four-letter word that is used daily, even though it is quite often misunderstood. It is the most powerful force of the universe; its energy and vibration bind everything together. It does not matter what life experiences are thrown at love because nothing can touch, harm, or reflect the powerful force of it. No experience—no matter how bad—can ever harm love. How is that possible? Well, it is possible because love is our universal eternal home in the soul of everything. I learned this as a child, and this is why I am sharing my experiences with you. My hope is that by sharing my experiences, others will then be encouraged to share theirs, too.

As a child, I called it my little "love balloon." I entered the physical world as a baby; everyone else meant nothing to me. I was unaware. As time went by and I became a child . . . and then a teenager . . . I came face-to-face with many different experiences—experiences no one should have to go through. I was mentally and physically abused. I was also starved and neglected. Ironically, these dark experiences helped shed an incredible light on my life. It took some time to realize it, but I was given the biggest gift life could have given me.

I had lost both my parents—my entire world at the time—and suddenly felt incredibly alone. I carried an unimaginable fear on my back. All of the material comforts, including food, as well as human love and contact had been taken away from me. I was isolated, cold, and physically stripped bare. My mind overflowed with total negative abuse. There I was at four years old, learning firsthand that adults had the power to abandon me, die, and abuse me. Yet through it all, I found the one precious gift that no one could touch, take, harm, or abuse . . . the real *me*.

The stuff inside of us—the stuff we can't see—is called essence. It is invisible to the naked eye and cannot be grabbed. We can spiritually feel it, however, because it touches our souls. We all have our own essence within us; everyone's essence is completely unique to them. As a child, I realized what my essence was—my own self-love. A calming feeling came over me as I understood that it would always belong to me. While we can share our life experiences with others on this planet however we'd like, our essence—our love balloons, so to speak—will only belong to us.

Years later, I attended college and enrolled in a counseling course. We were given an assignment regarding our family history.

Once we compiled our information, we had to share our backgrounds with the class. After sharing, I was told that *I* needed counseling! Okay, so that was the professor's personal opinion. She was drawing conclusions only based off my history of experiences inflicted by my abusers' own pain. To this day, that pain did and does not belong to *me*; I was just in the firing line. Looking back, I wish the professor had gotten to know me before passing judgment on a past experience and labeling me by my scarred childhood.

This has happened many times before. Luckily for me, people are starting to see me more now as the person I really am instead of how I could have turned out if I had given up hope on everything—including myself. By no means am I saying that counseling is bad; I'm just trying to show how easy it can be to be judged by an experience and then misunderstood, even by professionals. Remember, experiences are strung together to make up part of who you are, but they do not make up the *whole* you.

Most people react to a traumatic experience with shock, horror, anger—or all three emotions. They will look at someone who has gone through a particularly bad experience and think, *Oh, no! You must be damaged goods after that! You must have problems . . .* They do not attempt to see the real person who went through the ordeal. They suddenly do not know how to communicate with the person because they don't know how to relate. Mostly, though, they are afraid.

On the bright side, healing starts from the very moment any harsh experience occurs. It can take anything from a few minutes to a few hours to a few days, weeks, months, or even years. It all depends on the nature of the experience and whether any knowledge or details are missing. Naturally, it takes time, communication, listening, and understanding as much as possible about each detail that happened. Most importantly, the person going through the healing process needs to figure out what, within that situation, actually belongs to her or him and what belongs to the other party involved in the shared experience.

The power of love helped me to heal and gave me strength over many years to come to terms with why certain things happened to me the way they did. Down the road, I had a significant breakthrough when I met my childhood sexual abuser face-to-face. He was clearly in incredible pain; he had been carrying it for his whole life. But he wasn't suffering because of what he had done to me. He was suffering because of his own pain and what had been done to him in the past; that pain was still raw and had not yet been healed. My painful experience, in truth, was a reflection of his own pain—a pain that belonged to him, not me. It was at this point that I felt sympathetic for him. I was able to overcome what had happened in order to feel free and whole again. Sadly, he is still imprisoned in his own pain. After our encounter, I forgave him. In fact, I only felt love toward him. Some people would find that odd, I know, but without that experience I would never have learned about what it feels like to be hurt so badly.

These large, dramatic experiences eventually melt into smaller, less significant ones over time. They begin to shrink as our own awareness pieces together the bigger picture of what happened. We learn from all of our experiences, good and bad. They teach us about our personal strengths and weaknesses in a hands-on manner. My experiences, especially the one involving physical abuse, taught me about compassion, understanding, feeling, and seeing beyond the surface of specific actions. I learned that underneath any picture of the surface hides a bigger picture. *That* picture makes up the whole picture, and it is always experienced with love.

But the biggest problem that clouds the meaning of love is this: We are programmed from a young age into the materialistic side of love. We are taught through advertisements, television, and the media that love means gifts, price tags, chocolates, new clothes, pricey restaurant meals, diamond jewelry, vacations, cars, houses, and new kitchens—I could go on forever. Do you see our limited view of love? Is that what love truly means to you?

All of these examples have one thing in common: the feel-good factor. It's equivalent to placing a bandage on a cut to help heal it. Furthermore, the materialistic "love" items mentioned above are all bought with money. Sure, they can be great treats, but the truth is that they don't equal *real* love. Real love is not measured in gifts. Instead, love is a lesson measured in our experiences banks within our souls. It is a genuine smile or simply holding hands. It is cuddling on the couch. It is talking, communicating, and learning about each other. It is supporting, encouraging, and trusting. It benefits our spiritual and emotional growth and acknowledges our gifts from within.

And that's not all. Love is our essence. It shines our love of ourselves to others. We can't change people or their attitudes toward us. We also can't make anyone change their attitudes toward themselves or toward others. Only we, as individuals, have the ability to develop ourselves and grow in love. This is exactly why we experience many different variations of love in our lifetimes. No matter what it is, no matter how happy or sad we are, love can always be found. It has no preference.

Even though life sometimes seems harsh and black clouds cover whatever negative situation we find ourselves in like a thunderstorm, love is always shining its teaching and warmth on us. It may not always feel like it is, but there are always people around who care and support us in our times of need. The most important person who will always be there for you is yourself. *You* will never let you down, right?

Experiences come and go, but love will always be there—

especially when it comes from within. When you acknowledge your own love, you will then be able to acknowledge love from others. But there are times when some of us can be needy—sometimes without even realizing it. We become codependent to survive off of other people's love. This happens because we lose touch with our own love. We forget that it's even there because all of our focus and attention are on other people. This is a bad habit that potentially causes limited situations. Compare it to weeds popping up around a flower. Eventually, the flower suffocates and dies. We need to try and remember to stay attuned to ourselves first and foremost before we can begin to love others.

What does love mean to you? Do you acknowledge your own love? Think of love inside of you as your own eternal credit card. Again, you reap what you sow. How rich are you in your heart and soul? This internal balance is delicate; it has no relation to your physical bank or the job you do. It's credited simply by the meaning that you share and give in life.

Love is life; enjoy the school of learning about love. Let's hope it's catching so we enjoy love beyond the greeting cards, roses, and chocolates! They're a bonus, yes, but they're far from the meaning and truth of love's essence. Even better, we take love with us when we die. We take all of its knowledge, learning, and experiences of feelings. We should embrace our experiences, knowing they have deeper meanings than the experiences themselves.

Love has no boundaries or limitations; only physical people put these in place. Why? Let's step outside of the imaginary boundaries. Let's enjoy smiling and sharing love together. It is good for the heart and soul, and heck, it's free for all eternity! And if we're ever feeling negative or in a funk from which we simply can't get out of, it's always nice to remember that love is something no one can ever take away from us.

∞

SIX

Skeletons of the Earth

One winter's day, I moved from London to the countryside. *What a new adventure!* I thought. The country looked and smelled so different from what I had been used to back in London. While some folks would say the country offers plenty of fresh air, I noticed more of a slight odor that would come from a toilet. Oh, yes, the country is full of farms—farms and fertilizer. "Food of the earth," I've been told. Well, whatever the reason for it, it still stinks. I soon realized there was no getting away from it, either.

I was very excited about staying with actual blood relatives in the country. Growing up, family had meant various people in a group who all had different names. After I lost my parents, the scenes of my familiar world vanished into thin air. To this day, all I have left of my parents are my toys in my mother's laundry basket.

Once at the farm, I was immediately introduced to my relatives. *Hmm,* I thought. *I vaguely remember the face of the person who is standing in front of me—a face that once upon a time had visited in my kitchen back home*. It was a face that visited my mother a handful of times before she died. This face—a link in the chain with my mother—was apparently my sibling, or so I was told. *Wow*, I thought. *We have something in common*.

I felt a shy smile spread slowly across my face, unsure of how it would be received. The towering figure, the familiar face, patted me on the head. "Follow me . . ." he mumbled. I nodded and began to follow him obediently.

We walked up the path to the front door of a big farmhouse. The wind whistled through all the tiny cracks in the walls, sounding a bit like ghosts in song. Suddenly, the door slammed shut once we were fully inside. The wooden floorboards creaked eerily with each step we took. It reminded me of piano keys mirroring our steps. *Boom, boom, boom* went his heavy steps. They swallowed up my own—a mere whisper among the orchestra of everyone else's feet around us.

I nervously climbed up onto the wooden chair at the table, my warm breath making swirls in the air. My relatives paced anxiously around me, staring in my direction almost in an accusatory way. I started to feel confused. *What's going on?* I wondered.

Someone put the kettle on for a cup of tea. I sat there with my coat still firmly buttoned up to my neck, twiddling with the buttons. I was with family but this family felt so alien-like to me. Their voices chatted away with words I couldn't hear. It was like being underwater. I snapped myself out of my blurred state and focused on everyone's body language. I looked at their facial expressions. *Are they happy? Sad? Are they even pleased to see me?*

My excitement quickly faded as my internal questions were soon answered. No, they weren't pleased to see me at all. In fact, they considered me to be the dirt beneath their feet—the stench outside in the farmyard. To them, I was a game to play with, day and night.

I was an invisible intruder—a piece of their gold. And so the story slowly unfolded . . .

The money my dad had left to my mother—the money Mom left for me to survive after they were gone—now lay in the hands of one particular man. I would soon become a human credit card to him and the rest of his family. In exchange for the money, I would get a roof over my head. He, on the other hand, would get a fat wallet.

YET, I STILL SEE ME . . .

The sunshine shining outside reminded me of the games I used to play when life was simple and carefree. But in the rickety old farmhouse, I knew I'd start playing a different kind of hide-and-seek. I hid in the darkness and the shadows of the house, feeling like I was living in a grave. Days and nights became my living hell; the shadows of fear became my only friends. The smell of my own fear was my food, and the smile on my face eventually turned into stone. But there was one thing I constantly reminded myself: *Yet, I still see me . . .*

The days rolled into each other. The family members would shout at each other and throw the furniture around the rooms. I was in a war amongst relatives whom I did not know, or want to know—and the war was being waged against me. Afraid and alone, I'd curl my little body up into a ball. Again, I'd remind myself, *Yet, I still see me . . .*

The family never called me by my name. In fact, it would change daily, depending on their fiery tempers. "Come here, you little piece of shit!" they would often hiss at me. "Stand in the corner and watch us eat."

My tummy would growl, but not for food. I craved human

affection, like the cuddling my parents used to give me. Instead, I stood rigid like a statue and did as I was told. My body soon followed my face and it, too, turned to stone. I watched this family of monsters from behind my cave—my stone shell, the place I now called home. It was a makeshift shelter that I vowed would not let anyone penetrate.

Day in and day out, I stood there like a prisoner on guard. I watched them shovel mouthfuls of food into their mouths at every meal. My legs shook with fear under my shell. Slowly, so as not to draw attention to myself, I would pinch the skin on my hands to know that I was still there—underneath the gravestone that covered my body. *Yet, I still see me . . .*

I found myself living a slow death, feeling a small pang of dread when I woke up each day. Only my breath reminded me that I was still alive. I'd walk downstairs and wait for the man or his family to begin barking orders at me. Sure enough, the man stood up from the table when he saw me and began scraping his leftovers off of his plates and into a bowl.

"Sit on the floor!" he demanded as if I were a dog, pointing at the dirty floor. I fell heavily to my knees, exhausted and defeated. On all fours, I stared blankly at nothing, unsure of what would come next. The man threw the bowl of scraps down by my face. "Eat your food," he said wickedly. I didn't move. He forcefully pushed my head into the bowl, inches away from the leftovers. Suddenly, I visualized the time when I used to climb up onto my dad's knee and share his dinner with him. I kept the memory with me for as long as I could. *Yet, I still see me . . .*

I twisted my face around the bowl, trying to place the food in my mouth as best as I could; my hands no longer belonged to me. I could feel my body slowly slipping away. "Time's up!" he laughed, pulling my hair and making my whole body rise above the bowl.

The man's audience giggled with delight at the sight of me, helplessly dangling in midair. "You filthy animal! That's what you are!" he growled. He threw me against the dining room table and chairs. The others laughed and egged him on.

And so he continued. He grabbed me and flung me toward the table again. I was a rag doll in flight. I slammed against one of the chairs, hitting my head. My whimpers of pain were muffled by the family's shrieks of excitement. *Yet, I still see me . . .*

"Sit on the chair, you orphaned piece of crap!" the man ordered. "No one wants you! No one loves you! It's all your fault that Mother is dead. You ruined everything!" His anger and bitterness foamed out at me like a tidal wave—or like the angry screams of a rabid animal.

He slammed a glass of water in front of me to drink. My hands shook as I lifted the glass to my lips. Too frightened to actually be thirsty, I began drinking to appease him. He paced around me like a wolf stalking its prey.

Suddenly, one of the family members began throwing pots and pans against the wall and onto the floor. The man swung his head around to see what the commotion was about. They began to scream and shout about money, stress, and work. "It's all her fault!" one of them cried, pointing in my direction. I sat there, shocked and bewildered by the scene. Without notice, everyone stood up and walked out of the house, slamming the front door behind them.

It was just me and the man left in the kitchen. My heart began to pound with anxiety.

His eyes grew wide and dark. "My family just left because of *you*," he hissed. Then he focused on my glass of water, still half full. "Open your mouth!" he said, hovering over me. I did as I was told. Our eyes met; his had so much fire and rage in them. Then, without warning, he poured the glass of water down my throat. I spluttered to keep up. When I finished the glass, he slammed it on the table and stormed out of the room. Flinging open the front door, he stomped down the porch steps to go see where his family went.

Moments later, he returned, still angry as ever. He watched me without saying a word. Soon, I started to absentmindedly fidget as the pins and needles from not moving for so long made my hands and legs itch. He noticed that I was uncomfortable and glared at me. "Do you need to use the bathroom?" he asked.

I shook my head no. "I just—" I began.

He was not having any of it. With one fell swoop, he lifted me out of the chair by my clothes and threw me against the back door. "Use the outhouse that's up the path," he spat at me. "And don't even *think* about running away . . ."

By this time, it was cold and dark outside. I managed to find the outhouse at the bottom of the path. I opened the door and a wall of cobwebs plastered my face. I jumped out of fright. Taking a deep breath, I sat on the ice cold toilet, my legs dangling above the dirty floor. *C'mon* . . . I silently willed myself to go. I prayed. I even thought about screaming for help—maybe someone would hear me and come save me from the hell I was in? I also thought about running away even though the man had warned me against it. *What do I have to lose?* I wondered.

My thoughts of escape were soon dashed when I heard the familiar heavy booming steps coming up the path. My legs felt numb. Suddenly, the outhouse door swung open. "Well?" he shouted. "Have you gone yet?"

Embarrassed and self-conscious, I sat there and blurted, "Um, no . . ." My reply sounded fragile and far away, like it wasn't coming from me.

"No?" he repeated. "How dare you not do as you're told!?" He began swinging his fists, trying to make contact with my head. I scrambled to protect myself, but he got me once and I toppled into one of the walls of the outhouse.

That was just the beginning of many bathroom-related incidents. I soon learned how to go on demand, or at least pretend to.

A few days later, the man approached me with a beer and a cigarette in each hand. He sat down on a chair next to me and, without looking at me, announced, "I have a friend who will be staying with us for a few days. You better behave . . ."

His friend was welcomed into the farmhouse with laughter and a beer as soon as he arrived. The man's family embraced the guest as if he were part of the family, too. I couldn't believe how different everyone could be when it was just us. I hoped I would be treated fairly and as a human being during the visitor's stay.

It was getting late. I excused myself from the living room and headed toward my bedroom. I prayed I would get my first good night of sleep. Strangely, my prayers were answered.

A few days passed. Everyone in the family seemed to be enjoying themselves. The man's friend was having a good time, too. Even still, I made sure to keep my distance from the family, and especially the man. Nighttime became my peace—a refuge of the day. I'd rest my head on my pillow and stare outside the window at the moon shining in the sky. "Goodnight, moon," I would say. Then I would pull my thin blanket up around my shell—protecting the real me who no one could see or come after. *Yet, I still see me . . .*

With my bedroom door still ajar, I could hear the laughter coming from the man and his guest. Cigarette smoke swirled up the stairs and into my dingy room. I lay in my bed like a statue on guard, silently willing the day to be turned off by night. Something felt off compared to the previous nights. I held my breath and waited.

My eyes had almost closed when suddenly I heard footsteps outside my door. They stopped. When my eyes finally adjusted to the darkness, I saw the man standing beside me. My heart stopped. Immediately, he put his hands firmly across my mouth to silence any noise that I could make. I wanted to cry out for help but I knew no one would come to my rescue.

"I have to sleep in your bed," he said with a wicked grin. "My friend has my bed, and I have nowhere else to go . . ."

I felt my body begin to tremble with fear and tried to get out of the bed as fast as I could. But he was too strong and pushed me back down. "Stay where you are," he whispered. "We are sharing this bed."

I felt myself dying on the inside as I forced myself to became a statue again—rigid like a corpse. I needed to clear my head and focus on the one thought that got me through times of stress and abuse caused by this monster. *Yet, I still see me . . .*

He drunkenly fell to the floor as he attempted to climb into bed with me. Getting up, he unzipped his trousers and laughed. I closed my eyes and held my breath, waiting for the experience to be over. Now I silently begged for daylight to come; nighttime was no longer my solace. He moved his heavy body on top of me, squeezing out all of the air in my lungs. I tried to block out everything as he placed his hands all over me. I could not let my small shell crack under his massive weight.

Mentally, I escaped. I found myself standing in the corner of the bedroom, watching with disgust as he had his way with my four-year-old body. *Yet, I still see me . . .* I said over and over again in my mind, calming my nerves. I was safe in the corner. In fact, I felt nothing as he did whatever he wanted to do that night. Yes, I was invincible. Nothing he did could affect me. I looked out of the window at the moon; its round face looked down at me, almost twinkling. Morning would soon come.

He had only scratched the surface of my shell; my free will and choice had protected me well. Spiritually, I was able to find the key to unlock the physical chains that he had tried so hard to strangle me with. I was able to mentally travel to the safe place within my soul that even he could not see or harm no matter how hard he tried. That night, I learned that my free will and choice would protect me from evil for all eternity.

Morning arrived and the man was gone. The only trace left of him was a damp patch between my stone legs. I wiped myself dry and got up to go look in the mirror above the small bureau. I focused on looking through the surface stonewall of me—through the black and blue marks. And finally, I found her—the little girl I truly was. I saw the innocent girl my parents used to see. I smiled at the memory.

I walked out of the bedroom and sat quietly on the stairs, feeling my new armored strength deep inside my hands. Perhaps the family could only pretend to be happy for so long in the visitor's presence? I could hear them arguing and screaming at each other all over again.

But this day was different to the ones I had become accustomed to. As I listened to the commotion downstairs, I suddenly heard the front door fly open, the family stomp out, and then the door slam shut. *Not again* . . . I thought, peering over the banister. I heard the car start and drive away. Panic began to set in me once again. I braced myself for the unexpected, knowing it was just me and the man left alone once more . . .

I stayed silent and curled up in a ball on the landing behind the cupboards. Although the real me was already invisible to the man, I wanted my stone shell to be invisible, too. I wasn't sure how long my body could take the physical abuse anymore.

Many hours passed. I was too afraid to leave my hiding spot. But soon enough, he found me. He stood menacingly at the foot of the stairs with a wooden bat gripped tightly in his hands—his weapon of choice. Without warning, he began to fly about the various rooms. Even from the top of the stairs, I could smell his drunken breath as it floated up toward me and hit me in the face.

"Come down here!" he demanded, his voice full of rage.

Slowly, I edged out of my hiding place and walked down the stairs toward my abuser. Each step felt like a sword stabbing through my feet. As I neared the bottom step, he began swinging. I did all I could to dodge the erratic swings of the bat. But I wasn't fast enough. He grabbed my hair and lifted me off my feet, flinging me around the lower stairs. I could feel my stone legs crumble and flake as I was thrown into the living room and ordered to stand in the corner, facing the wall.

I had been hit so many times that my vision became blurry. Furthermore, the inside of the farmhouse had been hit so many times that we were both unrecognizable. Together, we made up a battlefield that had also been hit by an earthquake—my captor. I stood there, waiting. What else could I do?

The crazed man used the wooden bat to smash the TV and anything that was in his path. From the corner of my eye, I looked through the stained net curtains and focused on all the wildflowers swaying in the breeze. I concentrated on the lovely green grass. And in that moment, I wished that I were a flower—anything but the shell I was. *Yet, I still see me . . .*

But my attempt at thinking positive thoughts despite what I was going through were immediately dashed as the man drew the curtains closed, making the room so dark that we could hardly see a few inches in front of us. Now no one would know what was about to happen. He pulled off all my clothes so that I stood naked in front of him. *Yet, I still see me . . .* I repeated in my mind. *I can get through this.*

He ordered me to stand still and and face the wall again, his words angry like a boiling stew. He shouted every kind of abuse he could hurl at me, all the while flailing the wooden bat around the room.

The next game to come was a lesson in mathematics.

One. The wooden bat slammed into my stone back with such force that my legs buckled and I fell forward. This made him angrier. I didn't have time to feel the pain. It took all of my strength, physically and mentally, to stand like the statue that he liked. Attempting to gain my composure, I took a deep breath and made my stone frame rigid once again. *Yet, I still see me . . .*

Two. Another thump of the wooden bat etched the meaning of why I was getting pummeled this way. "You evil piece of shit . . ." he whispered into my ear, trying to get some kind of a reaction from me. *Yet, I still see me . . .*

Three. The bat was swung across my back again. On this strike, I felt my stone back become numb. Tears stung and overflowed from my eyes, but I did not make a sound. I did not want to give him the satisfaction of knowing he had broken me. I told myself that I just had to be strong enough to stand the force. *Yet, I still see me . . .*

Four. Yet, I still see me . . .

Five. Yet, I still see me . . .

The blood from my stone shell ran down my legs in a steady stream, making the bat slip and slide with each slam against my body. *Six. Seven. Eight. Nine. Ten. Eleven. Twelve*. The blood was now a pool around my feet. I couldn't feel anything. Over and over in my head I repeated the five words that kept me hanging on. Yet, I still see me . . .

Finally, the man tired himself out. I had been beginning to think this moment would never come. He dropped the wooden bat to the floor with a thud. I held my breath and waited for him to leave the room. When he did, I let out a tiny sigh of relief.

A few weeks later, the man and his family told me they had had enough of me; they were driving me back to Social Services. Like a credit card, I was at their limit—no longer useful to them anymore. I was placed back into the care system and they drove away without looking back. Meanwhile, I decided to hide that time in my life behind my stonewall frame. It would be my secret of how I found the real me inside me when I needed to discover myself the most.

As evil as that man was, he never truly found me or had me. He only touched the surface. What mattered most, my essence, had been protected by me—a stonewall of will, if you will. I kept the real me safe at all times with my inner courage and spiritual strength. I stared fear in the face and came out victorious on top. Loving myself helped keep me sane and, more importantly, alive.

∞

SEVEN

GUIDED AFTERLIFE TOUR: PLAYGROUND, GIFTS, AND SKILLS

Our bodies have come a long way since we were born. Think about all of the things they can do over time, and as we grow stronger and gain confidence in our individual skills. Take swimming, for example. I can swim with my feet still touching the floor of the pool. Hold on; let me explain! When I took swimming lessons as a child, my arms would do the breaststroke even though I had difficulties kicking my legs at the same time. I wasn't confident with my swimming abilities. But somehow, I managed to get away with my, uh, unique technique! My instructor never corrected me or yelled at me (although, I have a feeling she didn't know what I was doing). Besides, how was I supposed to swim twenty widths of the pool when *one* would have taken me the whole hour of the class?

When it came to swimming, slow, for me, was an understatement. But to keep up and not be left behind, "swimming" my way was the only thing I could come up with at the time. Being naïve, I thought the instructor would only be able to see my *surface* actions, not what I was (or wasn't) doing underneath the water with my legs. This example illustrates how we use parts of ourselves to cover up and hide other parts.

Today, I am confident to admit that I don't know everything. I am good at some things while other things need a little work. But this is why we have so many different activities to choose from in the playground of life, so to speak. If we all had the same skill sets and abilities, nothing would ever be a challenge; life would get boring pretty quickly. Like with any new activity, we must practice at it to become good. Think about learning to walk. We all fell over a lot until we worked out how to balance ourselves properly. Or think about riding a bike. Training wheels were great stabilizers to start us off so that we trust ourselves and build up our confidence levels.

Trust and confidence come hand in hand. Furthermore, think of balance as the regulator. Without trust, confidence, and balance, we tend to lose our judgment. This is also where ego takes over and we can become careless. Carelessness causes accidents because our confidence (when not combined with trust and balance) through memory of perfecting a skill leads us into a false sense of security. This is why we hear of accidents occurring that involve professionals in a particular field. Without trust, confidence, and balance, our connections with all of our senses can get lost. In turn, we do not listen to our inner guidance; only the *doing* factor becomes important. And that's when we get hurt.

Being a medium allows me to be aware of my trust, confidence, and balance at all times. My *beingness* reminds me that my afterlife body is here, too, and that I need to treat it with the utmost respect. With each reading I do for someone, I treat that reading as if it is my first. I am always aware of the three safety points. I am able to work from my heart and receive guidance as I need to; my ego never takes over.

But you don't have to be a medium to gain the benefits of knowing how to juggle trust, confidence, and balance. Practice makes perfect. Try tuning in to and listening to both of your bodies. When you do so, you can fully enjoy activities within your comfort zone. You begin to understand what your capabilities are. There's a saying that goes like this: "We can only do our best." But I like to think of it as "We can only do something to the best of our *abilities*." Again, if we are aware of the three links of trust, confidence, and balance, we are able to enjoy what we do to the best of our abilities without feeling out of our personal depths. Basically, it all comes down to speaking up about what our abilities and capabilities are. It never feels good to be overwhelmed or pushed into situations that feel uncomfortable for us.

The playground, so to speak, in which we live on earth always connects us with the complex doingness and beingness that we are: Our doingness makes up our physical bodies and our beingness makes up our afterlife bodies. When combined, we all make up neat little packages—both bodies are always connected. As I've mentioned before, we never leave the afterlife home. Our physical bodies (doingness) simply forget about where we came from, and we only see the physical side of life. However, we experience days when we suddenly have hunches or gut instincts inside ourselves. These feelings are trying to remind us about the wholeness we truly are—packages of two halves.

I am able to talk to and see afterlife people because they are not dead. None of us are, if you think about it, and we do not have to wait until we let go of our physical bodies to realize this. After all, we do not hold on to our old vehicles once we are done with them. They are just modes of transportation used to navigate around the world so that we can visit the many places in which we want to see and explore. Really, this is no different to what we use our physical bodies for. *We are not our physical bodies*.

Remember, our real bodies cannot be seen by our physical eyes. They have been forgotten about, almost as if they are a part of a dream while we are having life experiences on earth. We only remember our real bodies once we have left our physical vehicles, so to speak. And this takes me to the word "afterlife." Most people take this word at face value, meaning the afterlife is the life we have *after life*. It must be about when we die, right? Well, no. Some of you may have expected me to only talk about the afterlife of where dead people live. Instead, I have talked a lot about life here on earth. To me, this is where all the confusion lies. We worry ourselves sick wondering what goes on after we leave here. To put it in the simplest of terms, the truth about the word afterlife . . . is life.

The word, "after," is not the end of one life and the beginning of the next. After indicates a continuation—a continuation of *life*. One life experience follows the next life experience; it is a continuation with no gaps or ends. While it seems like we experience an end, this is not the case in the grand scheme of things. But where does this illusion come from? Why do we think the way we do? It comes from our language and various figures of speech. It also stems from not really having the right words to understand things properly. For example, our parents always told us, "Finish up your dinner . . ." or our teachers said, "Write a story with a beginning, a middle, and an end." These phrases we learned during our childhoods are where it all begins.

If we could remember our whole lives instead of just the physical parts, we would not be so upset about death, in general. We would not be afraid of the unknown because we would know what to expect—or at least understand it and know that it isn't a scary process. We would remember the truth that our loved ones have not died, after all; they have just finished using their body vehicles. Their real bodies continue on to another life experience. Just because we can't see them with our physical eyes or hear them with our physical ears, it doesn't mean they are not around us. They are always around if we want them to be.

When my grandmother was close to death, I visited her to help try and make her legs feel better using a holistic approach. She never knew about what I do or that I can talk to "dead people." She was brought up in the Christian faith, and believing what she believed made her happy. While I was healing my grandmother's legs using comfort and warmth, she suddenly spoke up. "What is that light in the corner of the room?" she asked. "Oh, how lovely! All of my relatives have come to visit me, including my husband!"

I smiled, knowing what she was seeing even though they weren't physically in the room. She was connecting with all of her friends, relatives, and even her husband who had died many years ago. She was seeing them with her afterlife body eyes—eyes she always had. The only difference was that she was so used to seeing with her physical eyes that, up until now, she thought and believed they were the only ones she had. Yet, at this moment, she remembered her afterlife body eyes. The connection and strength of her physical body was getting weaker, giving her the chance to see the whole of life while still in her present state. In those few moments, she could see the truth that her loved ones had never left her. After their deaths, my grandmother's physical eyes led her to believe that they were gone forever to some distant land referred to as heaven.

When my grandmother eventually joined her loved ones, we all gathered together in the church to celebrate her and to acknowledge all of her life experiences. As I looked around the crowded church, I smiled as I saw more than just the people in their physical bodies. Yes, my grandmother's discarded body/vehicle was in the coffin at the front of the church for everyone to pay respects to. But perched on a chair next to the coffin was my grandmother—the real her—grinning away with her arms outstretched. "These folks are all my family members and friends!" I heard her say. She looked very happy, well, and alive. And it was at this point that she looked directly at me and gave me the biggest smile ever, realizing she had not died, after all, and was now free to use her afterlife body however she wanted to. She had finally remembered the truth.

Dead people are not a mystery. They are only made a mystery because our physical eyes are not trained to see them. If we practiced using our afterlife body eyes, eventually we would be able to see them. But we tend to be too busy, skeptical, or both. Sadly, most of us hear, read, or watch fabricated and sensationalized ghost stories in books and in movies; we are taught that we should be afraid of dead people. Dramatic stories are more exciting to believe than the truth; the truth is not so dramatic because it is normal.

Our extreme lack of knowledge is what creates the mystery that surrounds the afterlife. Sadly, a large part of the allure has to do with business and making a quick buck. I understand that we all need money because that is how the world is, but I feel that the quality of our work should be based on our experiences of heart and truth, not the drama and labels of advertisements and false promises. I have been reluctant to share what I do with others because I exercise my craft from the heart. I let my work guide me; I definitely do not go looking for it. I am just a channel in which my work is expressed. It is only now that I am showing the world I exist purely for those who need a signpost.

Dead people are basically the same as you and me. To be honest, people in their physical bodies, at times, scare me more than people in their afterlife bodies. Why? In our physical bodies, we have so many unexposed layers and we work hard to cover up things we don't want others to know. We never see what we truly get. We're all a bunch of confusing puzzles. With afterlife people, however, what we see *is* what we get. We always know where we stand. Dead people—or *life people*, as they should be called—are fun and full of character. Usually, whatever kind of character they had while on earth is the same in the afterlife. I have communicated with talkative people, quiet people, shy people, confident people, expressive people, grumpy people, and happy people. Catch my drift, here? These folks sound a lot like the people on earth, right?

They do all the things we do while on earth but they do much more and they're better at whatever they do, too. They have houses if they want them. They eat if they want to. (However, they know their afterlife bodies do not need to eat to survive.) They have music halls and play games. They get their hair done and wear clothes. Some of the children I have seen play with bricks, ride bikes, and have all the toys we have on earth. If you think about it, why do you think toys are invented on earth for children in their physical bodies? We have played with them before! In fact, anything that is invented on earth is not new and is already used in the afterlife. This is why when some children are born, they have amazing talents and gifts. Some of them can naturally play the piano by the age of two even though their physical parents can't play at all. These kids brought their gifts to earth with them.

The afterlife playground is extremely busy, colorful, and complex, to say the least, much like the world we live in today. Furthermore, people who have afterlife bodies are very similar to people in their physical bodies. So why are we still so afraid of dead people? Afterlife people used to share their life experiences with us, traveling together in our physical vehicles. They lived with us and never scared us then. They help and guide us when we need them. We should embrace them and encourage them to interact with us.

Once people leave their physical bodies and have gone back home—once they remember their whole, real lives—they want so much to be able to share their new experiences with us. In fact, they begin to get creative in their ways to show us, or prove to us, that an afterlife exists. And this is where people like me come into play. Afterlife people use those who can see and talk to them to the best of their abilities. They also do whatever they can to try and get our attention. We shouldn't interpret these moments as spooky or frightening, but it can feel that way at times—especially when we do not understand enough about the afterlife. Again, we are so programmed to separate everything instead of connecting it all up. We tend to make our connections very selectively.

If an afterlife person can't get our attention, they may choose to try and communicate with us through our dreams. If this connection does not work, they can attempt to use the physical side of life. For example, they may move your car keys or random objects in your house. This isn't to scare us; it's to let us know that they are well, alive, and have arrived home safely.

I moved into my house approximately nine years ago. Having a big family, we tend to go through a lot of toilet paper. On one particular day, I had bought a pack with four rolls in it. I left the toilet paper on my bureau in my bedroom and went about my daily routine. The next day, I went into the bathroom. When I reached for the toilet paper, I saw that it was all gone. "What did they do with it? Eat it?" I mumbled under my breath, annoyed. I called down to my children to pass me the spare pack I had left in my bedroom the day before. Of course, I heard the usual moans together with heavy footsteps up the stairs.

"It's not here, Mom!" one of my kids cried out.

"Yes, it is," I replied, taking a deep breath. "I only put it there yesterday."

"No, Mom. It really isn't!" my child responded.

I sighed, utterly confused. There I was, sitting on the throne, while I had to wait for them to run down to the store to buy another pack. About twenty minutes later, they returned. Finally, I was able to get on with my day.

I searched my bedroom from top to bottom, knowing the four-pack had to be *somewhere*. I had seen the package on my bureau that morning when I was getting dressed! After much searching, I gave up. Clearly, the rolls had disappeared.

The next day, I woke up to find the four-pack on my bureau as if it had been there all along. Now we had a lot of toilet paper! I rolled my eyes and grinned, thinking to myself, *Thank you for getting my attention, but will you please leave me with at least one roll of toilet paper next time?*

Another example of when someone from the afterlife was trying to communicate with me involves music. I had a CD player in my bedroom. One day, I was alone in the house, puttering around downstairs. Suddenly, the CD player upstairs in my room started to play! The music began to get louder and louder as if someone was turning the volume up. At first, I became alarmed; it was late and I didn't want to disturb the next-door neighbors.

I ran upstairs to turn the volume down only to realize that the CD player was already switched off. That's when I knew that someone from the afterlife wanted my attention. I wasn't afraid; I know they never want to harm me. But these encounters are often unexpected—and that's what makes me jumpy sometimes. Now that these things happen often and I know *why* they happen, I smile. I'm happy that they are stopping in to say hello. They remind me that they are still here.

Another personal anecdote illustrates how we all share life as one. At times, my house can be *very* active with the people coming and going. And I don't mean just with physical people. The afterlife ones come and go as they please, too. While we all share my house in the literal sense, that is not what I am talking about when I say we all share life as one. Let me explain . . .

My family once experienced a fire in our house. It had started in my bedroom around the time I went through a stage of lighting a candle every night before I went to bed. On this occasion, I forgot to blow it out. (I thought I had lit a tea light candle, which burns itself out automatically.) Suddenly, my daughter burst into my room. "Morning, Mom!" she said. Then she sniffed the air, adding, "It smells in here."

We both looked over at the candle, which clearly had not gone out on its own. In fact, it was smoking from the oil in it. In a panic, my first reaction was to immediately blow it out. But no matter how hard I tried, I couldn't get the darn thing to go out. Thinking quickly, my daughter ran and retrieved a cup of water to attempt to douse the flame.

Well, what happened next scared the life out of us both. The candle blew up in flames, catching my blinds on fire, too. In seconds, the flames spread up along my window. Then the burning blinds fell onto my bed, which has silk covers on it. *I need to get the kids out of this house now!* I thought.

Grabbing the children, we ran outside and piled into my car, all of us still in our pajamas. I used my cell phone to call the fire department, and soon they dealt with putting out the fire. As we watched the firemen battle the blaze, I looked up at my bedroom window. Looking through the window with my physical eyes, I feared the worse. My bed had been pushed up next to the window.

I also had posters all over my walls. Clothes had been drying on hangers on the window frame. My heart sank as the flames engulfed my material possessions.

Eventually, the firemen told us it was safe to go back inside *after* one of them yelled at me for pouring water on a candle. How was I supposed to know that was bad? I had never been told how to put out a burning candle before! If blowing it out didn't work, what else was I supposed to do? Apparently, I should have put a wet tea towel over it to smother it. So now, by experience, I know what to do. (Hopefully, I never have to test out my newfound knowledge!)

We braced ourselves for what we were about to walk into. To my surprise, the place didn't look as ruined as I thought it would be! The walls were a bit black and smoky, sure, but the only damage that was really done was to the window frame and glass. Even the blinds falling on the bed caused a cigarette burn-size hole! My clothes hadn't caught alight, and neither did any of my posters. However, the glass in the double glazing window got so hot that it cracked inside itself into a million pieces.

. . . This is why I love the connection with my afterlife body and that of my family and friends in the afterlife. They are around to support and guide us, not to frighten us. I truly believe that they helped keep my family safe that day. We should have been left with much less, but we weren't. In fact, after a few coats of fresh paint and a new window, my bedroom looked as good as new.

That is not the only time my family and I were saved by people from the afterlife. As I mentioned before, our loved ones who have moved on still check on us from time to time. They're still around. If we pay close attention, we can sometimes feel their presence.

One day, we were all in the car; I was being driven with my children in the backseat while my youngest was in her car seat. A woman named Lisa called my cell phone, wanting to book a reading with me at a later date. As we spoke, I suddenly felt a strong connection and vibration in my link with the afterlife. I gathered my thoughts and said very calmly into the phone, "Lisa, I have to go. I think I'm about to be in the middle of a car crash . . ."

In seconds, the car ran over metal signposts and crashed into a bridge, spinning around. I had no control of the steering wheel. During the whole ordeal, no one heard or felt a thing. It was as if our physical bodies had been momentarily turned off. A strange sense of calm, peace, and silence took over. It was not until the car came to a complete stop that the sound had been turned back on. Miraculously, no one was hurt.

Witnesses who had seen the crash take place came running to help us. They expected the worst. When we all got out of the car, unharmed, they were shocked. My youngest daughter, still in her car seat, was smiling. My other children, also unaware of the severity of what had just happened, were confused as to what all the fuss was about.

Someone had called an ambulance even before our car had stopped. When I tried to calm everyone down, saying we really were all fine, they just stood there, dumbfounded. Honestly, that split moment when we had no control—when we were experiencing what our afterlife bodies felt like as our physical ones were going through a traumatic time—was truly a magical experience.

Dead people are nothing to be scared of when we understand life. After all, we're not afraid of the people we share our lives with now, are we? Why should we suddenly become frightened of them because we can no longer physically see them with the eyes we once saw them with before? If you really wanted to use your afterlife eyes, you would then see them like I do. You would also realize that death is simply a continuation of life.

Our playground of life is shared by us all, no matter what side of the fence we are on. When someone says he or she saw a dead person floating down a flight of stairs or walking through walls, that person is only seeing an afterlife person from the physical side of life—not the whole picture. On the flipside, when that afterlife person was having life experiences on earth, he or she may have not seen any stairs or walls, just open fields. Just because we can't physically see something does not mean it is not there. We all experience life as we come to know it. We may be on the same page but we're focusing on different pictures . . .

Our lives are for us to enjoy and explore with everyone regardless of if they have physical bodies or afterlife bodies. Dead people live and enjoy life just like we do. My afterlife friends have only looked out for me and my family in love. I have never known any of my afterlife-related experiences to be spooky or scary, as the media describe. Despite the labels used in books and big screen movies, all I know is I feel safe when I am in the company of afterlife people. They have no hidden agendas. Like I said, what we see is what we get in truth and love with them. I think I can live with that.

∞

EIGHT

Does Death Hurt?

I am aware that death, as a topic, is a complex subject. Everyone has their own personal beliefs about it; we have all had different experiences dealing with it. But does death hurt? My short answer is no. While life has many layers, death has just as many. This makes sense because death is simply part of life's cycle of continuation.

As I've mentioned before, we all have two bodies to create one whole package. Both bodies have a story to tell about any situation or circumstance that life offers us as a whole to experience. We may *believe* that we experience different situations and convince ourselves that we did not order this or that experience within the layers of our thoughts, but in actuality we did and do.

The Waiting Room of Life

Our thoughts have a tendency to run away with us. We often act out situations before we have experienced them. Have you ever made an appointment to see your dentist, and you had to book your appointment weeks or even months in advance because that was when the next available appointment was open? We wonder what will happen during that window of time. If we have toothaches or mouth pain, we may stress out even more while we wait to finally be checked out. Or sometimes we may be scheduling an appointment for a routine procedure, but the waiting process makes us start to *think* we suddenly feel some other kind of pain going on. A lot of times, these aches and pains are just in our heads.

How many of our illnesses stem from our thoughts and fears? One thing's for certain; our thoughts have the ability to affect how we feel. They can also mimic actual illness symptoms. In a way, our thoughts play a big part in our overall mental health. They act like a valve, or a thermostat, in the many layers of our reactions toward illness and waiting rooms, in general. It is at these times that our bodies feel slower and more rundown. We are not operating at one hundred percent. When we slow down, we are able to connect more with our feelings and thoughts. When we are well, we tend to run away from them or ignore them because we become too busy with the many other things we have to do. Perhaps feeling a little under the weather is actually a blessing in disguise every now and then?

Now it's time for a few math equations. Don't panic; they're easy to understand. *I* = *Illness* (focused on one body), where as *WE* = *Wellness* (balanced with the two bodies). When we think and act on our own with only our physical bodies, the *I* comes into play. That is when we can talk ourselves into feeling and thinking things that are not real or actually happening. Do you see why it's important to try and balance or at least get in tune with both bodies?

Creation and intentions are very powerful. Think of our thoughts as the plans and drawings to what we create and go on to experience. But we also have the power of memory. Memory experiences can actually feel more real than the original experience. Why is this? Well, first experiences tend to be about survival, not about feelings. It is not until we have survived a situation that we then begin to feel something about it. When we connect a memory to an experience, all of our feelings come flooding back and the experience then becomes imprinted in our minds.

"Survival" is a word we use to experience a particular event; it is comparable to having all of our blood drained from our veins. Once the experience is over, we suddenly experience a huge rush (feelings) because all of our blood is going back into our veins. If someone were to ask us about the experience, we would more likely give details pertaining to the blood rushing back into our veins and the feeling we got when that was happening than we would about the process of our blood draining out. Our memories play a big part in this process as it gathers all other similar experiences and combines them. We end up with a detailed log, so to speak, of many experiences in one!

The next time you hear two people communicating with each other, just listen. More than likely, one person will share a experience that will trigger the other person's memory into sharing his or her own somewhat related experience. This is the power of the memory, which can expand a situation or belittle one, depending on the amount of related (or entirely unrelated) experiences people who are communicating may have.

Have you ever played the game where a group of people sit in a circle and one person starts off a sentence by whispering it to the person next to him or her? By the time the sentence is said to the last person, the sentence has usually changed into something entirely different from the original statement. It's the same thing with the media. Facts and figures are often vague while details are exaggerated to make for juicier reading. These examples show how our minds interpret different information from all over the place. Eventually, we collect layers upon layers of facts, figures, and hearsay to draw our own conclusions.

There is never a straight line that goes from Point A to Point B when it comes to our experiences. If anything, it's more a zigzag line of life. This fluctuation gives life its many intricate layers and helps provide some kind of meaning to the many different experiences that we have. "Personal" is a relevant word to use. We all feel and react to various situations, even if we experience the same situation with someone else. No matter what, however, our reactions, thoughts, and memories pertaining to these experiences will always differ from the reactions, thoughts, and memories of others.

I remember getting scolded when I was living in the children's home because a bunch of kids and I had gone to the shops and stolen some candy. (This was a luxury to us; we hardly ever got sweets except for a Bourbon biscuit at Christmastime.) Curiosity got the best of us, and we all felt brave to each steal one candy each. We were naïve then and didn't realize there would be severe consequences because of our actions. Before we knew it, the police were called. Soon after, we were all bundled into two police cars and taken back to the children's home.

We all waited anxiously in line in the hall while the policemen told the staff what had happened. After the staff members were clued in, we were ushered into the sitting room. We all stood close together, pushing against each other as we stood in line. Lucky for me, I was only four years old; I was the smallest and didn't really understand what was going on. I hid my little body amongst all the other kids, frightened of the big men with hats and uniforms on.

My point is that we all did the same thing: We stole candy from a store. We all took part in this experience, but the way *I* felt about it was reflective of my age, my attitude, my feelings, my outlook, my understanding of what we did, etc. How any of the other children felt about the same situation was completely different and based on how they viewed what had happened. Some felt angry, some felt rebellious, some felt proud, and some found it funny. Even though we shared an experience, we all felt differently about it in the end. However, that particular experience was logged into everyone's memory banks that day. I have a feeling that some of those children decided they would never steal again after that! See? Life is about lessons—some good, some bad—constantly being learned.

When we feel empowered by a situation, we go on to do more. We experience an adrenaline rush of sorts, and then concentrate on trying to recapture the initial feeling we had. In truth, we experience different layers of feelings. A trickle of feelings may not impact us much, but a rush of feelings can. We are impacted on many internal levels within the many layers that make us who we are. While one experience may have a rush effect on one person, the same experience could have a trickle feeling effect on another. Our feelings help us decide on what we want to create, reenact, or recreate in our minds. Our feelings play a huge role when it comes to how we interpret the world from the physical side of the fence.

While the afterlife side is similar to the physical side (remember the playground), it is also very different. Our afterlife bodies do not have to process a bunch of layers—layers that somewhat resemble the steps of a pyramid, if you think about it. Picture each experience we become a part of as a different step of a pyramid. Combined, these steps make up the layers of all that we feel and process about an experience. Our afterlife bodies do not have to go through this process.

Instead, our afterlife bodies are equivalent to being at the top of a pyramid. When we are in them, we can see all of the layers, how they work, why an experience happened, and what the purpose of it was. This insight allows our afterlife bodies to aid our physical bodies on earth in having multi-layered lives. Our afterlife bodies already know they can have all of that in an instant; they know and feel the bigger picture because they see from the top looking down on the wholeness of what is going on.

Sometimes, I wonder if the ancient pyramids were built as an example to show us the truth about ourselves and our intentions—to help us better understand our creation. I think of them as simple life experience tools to symbolize the wholeness of who we are. But it's easy to forget such simple truths. Perhaps that's why pyramids were built so grand and solid. Seeing them in all their greatness would prevent us from forgetting the message of seeing and remembering the truth.

Obviously, pyramids are not hidden gems; they are all over the world for people to visit and admire at their will. But if you enter one, you will see that what is on the *inside* is a lot more intricate and valuable. Metaphorically speaking, the hidden chambers and tunnels are like our internal physical sides of our bodies. They hold physical life. The outside, however, is naked to the world. On the outside, everything looks the same; everything is equal. When you go inside, you open your eyes to a lot more—details and information you wouldn't be able to see or understand by simply looking at the pyramid from the outside.

Have you ever heard the expression, "a bird's-eye view"? It all has to do with perspective. If we are standing on the center steps of our proverbial pyramid, our view is limited, both up and down. If we're standing at the bottom of the pyramid, we may not be able to see the top. If we are at the top, we get a much bigger picture of everything around us; that's why birds have an advantage when they're flying in the sky. Oftentimes, the view we have and our perspectives only allow us to see *parts* of the wholeness of what life is. The limitations we have from being on the lower steps, so to speak, cause us to pass judgment, create assumptions in our minds, and waste precious energy on unnecessary guesswork.

Our judgment and various ways of measuring experiences are tools with which we use to create meaning out of the bits and pieces of information we receive. As humans, we are programmed to analyze things by size and measurements. Take cooking in our kitchens, for example. We measure out our ingredients to create whatever it is we want to cook—the whole. When we take all of the different ingredients into account and acknowledge the fact that life is multi-faceted, only then can we take our aprons and enjoy life for what it is as a whole.

But back to the main topic at hand: death. You're probably wondering how it can't possibly hurt, right? While our physical bodies have nerve endings and feel a plethora of different sensations at any given time, we need to remember that our afterlife bodies do not need nerve endings. They don't feel pain. Sensitivity and pain, in general, are feeling indicators our physical bodies use to help us gauge different experiences and then put them into memory. Our physical bodies can differentiate between hot and cold water. Furthermore, when our physical bodies feel ill, our nerve endings send out warning signals.

Our afterlife bodies, on the other hand, interpret things from the perspective of a bird's-eye view. They know and feel the whole picture. They know they are safe and will not feel any pain. Most importantly, our afterlife bodies know they are real. And while we are in our physical bodies, our afterlife bodies act as shadows. They protect us and guide us, as appropriate, waiting in the wings until it's time for us to discard our physical vehicles.

Leading up to the time of death, our physical bodies may feel their nerve endings even more than they are used to. But the closer to death our bodies get, the more relaxed and calm they begin to feel. (Remember how I felt in the middle of my car accident?) This is all part of a transfer process. At first, we consume all of our energy and thoughts as we try to regulate our physical bodies. During the transfer process, however, we slowly start to transfer ourselves into our real afterlife bodies. This is why when someone is ill or close to death, we can physically see that they are with us, but if we look closely, it becomes apparent that they are not *really* there. They seem to be somewhere else . . . distant . . . transitioning.

As the transfer process continues, the physical body—the vehicle or shell—becomes vacant and empty. Think of it as taking the necessary time to move from your old home to a much nicer one. Our consciousness, or our beingness, moves from our physical bodies to reside back into our original afterlife bodies—the true bodies of who we are. This is why we hear about many near-death experiences. People who are on the brink of death connect with their afterlife bodies for a brief moment. They say they feel like they are at the top of a pyramid; they can see the wholeness of life from a new perspective. But they are brought back to their physical bodies for whatever reason. After a near-death experience, most people are not afraid to die. The physical body still struggles with understanding this concept. It has forgotten what the afterlife is like.

The symptoms our physical bodies feel will depend on our various layers. All series of layers are unique to each individual. This uniqueness can make the transition period different for everyone, but generally speaking, it is an easy process that does not hurt. Once the transition process is complete, our afterlife bodies are then able to see both bodies as they truly are. And when the metamorphosis is realized and understood, we are able to fully let go of our physical vehicles. It is at this point that we also realize we were never our physical bodies in the first place; those were just our vehicles to get around while on earth.

Remember, our afterlife bodies do not experience pain. Pain is for the physical side of the fence. However, if ever we are in an altered state of mind, our physical and afterlife bodies may play tricks on us as they connect and communicate with each other in various ways. For example, I once took my daughter to get four baby teeth removed; she needed braces. Once she was put under with anesthetics, she was fast asleep and no longer aware of her physical body. I went into the waiting room until the procedure was done.

Suddenly, I heard the most awful screams coming from my daughter. I became confused and worried, not being in the operating room or knowing what was going on. It sounded like she was being tortured. *I thought she wasn't supposed to feel anything?* I wondered. Panic began to set in as her screams continued. Shortly after, the dentist came over to tell me how she had done. "Why was my daughter screaming?" I demanded. The dentist reassured me that my daughter felt nothing during the surgery. Her own fears and anxious thoughts she had created in her mind had caused this bizarre reaction. It's the physical body's reaction to a memory or fear about something. I wasn't sure if I bought the dentist's answer. When my daughter was coherent enough for me to talk to her, I asked her about the screaming and if she had been in lots of pain.

Her reply surprised me. She said she felt nothing during the procedure. In fact, she didn't remember screaming at all. She thought she had simply fallen asleep. You see, just because our physical bodies are reacting as if we are in pain, the truth of the situation can be entirely different. The memories of our nerve endings have the ability to reenact an experience for us whether we're conscious or not. Our physical bodies experience the feelings while our afterlife bodies take in everything else.

It doesn't matter what kind of death someone from the afterlife shows me that he or she experienced—a natural death, a sudden illness, a car crash, a murder, suicide, hanging, drowning—I always see the same thing at the time of transition: two bodies. I see the physical vehicle body that experienced the death and the real afterlife body standing next to it. When afterlife people share their experiences with me, it is a lot like being shown a video and talking about it.

In a way, the video clip analogy makes a lot of sense. Our physical bodies are a projection of us—an experience captured on film to watch and possibly learn from. Naturally, when I first began seeing these transitions, I felt uncomfortable. I was looking at everything from a physical perspective. But I soon trained my eyes to view the experiences with my afterlife eyes. When I did that, I was able to notice how much peace and calm surrounded the transitions. I was seeing the bigger picture.

Again, all of our experiences as a whole help make us who we are, not just one particular experience. The afterlife people I have communicated with are free, very much alive, and well to share their stories with me. We must realize that only when the mask of death is taken off, we can begin to understand the continuous journey of life. It is a journey that is much more enjoyable when we embrace it. If we all understood that life is, indeed, a continuation and we never lose our essence, death would be celebrated the same way in which we celebrate birth.

Death is generally a peaceful transition, but it can be a shock to the system. Think about how you feel when people jokingly jump out at you when you least expect it. You suddenly jump and your heart immediately begins to race. But once you realize that no harm has been done and that there is no threat to you, you are able to relax. This fear is an intrinsic flight-and-flee mechanism; we just need to be prepared for whatever is going to happen to us. If we do not have the chance to be prepared, it can be a bit of a shock. People who die go to a healing place—a place that is a bit like our hospitals. There, they have a chance to adjust to their new afterlife bodies with all their deceased loved ones around them.

Our outlook toward death depends on how we personally feel about it and what our motives are for feeling the way we do about it. Is it about the transition or is it about letting go of our physical bodies? The whole transition becomes much easier when we realize that our loved ones who have already crossed over will be there to guide us as we need them. They will welcome us with open arms as they did when they had their physical bodies.

Don't think about beginnings and ends or tops, middles, and bottoms. Try to embrace the fact that death is just a *continuation* of life. What we feel about it lies within the many steps and layers of life. Our thoughts tend to mirror our personal experiences and our personal perspectives despite the fact that we may share hundreds or thousands of similar experiences with other people. If we practice using both of our bodies as a whole, we will be able to truly see and know so much more than what we see and know on the surface in our physical bodies.

Death does not hurt because we live on to tell the story.

∞

NINE

Questions and Answers

Over the years, giving readings and receiving messages from the afterlife enlightened me to more "behind the scenes" knowledge, as I like to call it—a perspective of this world into the next. Entering the world of those who have passed before us gave me a better understanding of how they now live. As I've said a few times already, it's not that different to the way we live on earth. The only difference is that afterlife people have more freedom and unlimited possibilities.

By conducting readings, I was privileged to receive and share some very humbling messages of truth, understanding, and forgiveness. The more I learned from the afterlife people, the more I wanted to know. I wanted to know about the big secret of death and the truth of what it's like to transition to the other side of the fence. To this day, I keep asking questions to learn as much as I can about the afterlife. This is a continuous journey for me.

Just because I can communicate with the afterlife doesn't mean I am any different than anyone else. Like you, I go about my life making mistakes here and there because that's what we do. It's how we learn. We are faced with many choices so that we can map out our lives with various twists and turns. Some paths may even send us back to where we began! Life is forever moving forward and changing; we simply have to adapt and go along for the ride. But this is also why asking questions, no matter how small or silly they may seem, gives us pieces of knowledge to help us understand more of what we are all about and why we are here. Our questions help us to open up ourselves to see and find out the whole of *who* we are, not just the small part we show the world and the people we share life with.

Our life experiences ultimately teach us to find the courage and strength to be ourselves and to be brave enough to be our own truths with open, inquisitive minds. As a child, I was conditioned to believe that growing up in different religions made me a *walking evil sin!* I thought that God was on a throne—unapproachable. I felt like I wasn't good enough to be in his presence. In fact, I didn't think I could go into the church unless I put on the right clothes. I started to question religion in my heart, trying to find out my own truth that felt right in my soul, not necessarily in my mind.

If God was so loving and forgiving, why would he be so bothered by what I dressed like? I mean, isn't it supposed to be about who I am, not what I look like? I am more than my clothes; they just cover me up in layers. Ironically enough, we are taught from a young age to cover up our feelings and our inquisitiveness, too. I began to wonder, if *God* would not accept me in certain clothes, how would *I* ever learn to accept me? How would the people around me accept me for who I am? More so, how could I learn to equally accept others?

I can tell you this: Being inquisitive, observing others, and asking questions has gotten me into trouble at times. We are taught to keep quiet and keep such questioning to ourselves. But I chose to be me from a young age. I swam against the waves, so to speak. And while it has been a tough swim, it has been worth it. I figured out how to open my mind to the feeling that there is more to life than what we see in our physical world—*much* more.

Over time, I learned that God or whomever or whatever you believe in, is approachable. That spiritual being is just like you and me with feelings. Feelings create thoughts that create questions. Doing the work that I do taught me that when we die, we don't become holy, per se. We're still the same as we were in our physical bodies with all of our character intact.

I remember one reading I did that involved two participants. One of them started writing down the message for the other. During the reading, an elderly man came through with a Victorian cap on, but he wasn't for either of the participants. I politely told him that he would have to wait; it would be his turn next. Upset with my response, he crossed his arms and glared at me as if to say, "How dare a woman tell me I have to wait my turn!" You see, when he lived on the earth, women were seen and not heard. He was extremely irritated by what I had told him that he even stamped his foot on the floor before storming off. Regardless of his childish behavior, that man did make me smile and he taught me a bit more about life after leaving our physical bodies. This special reading showed me how full of character we are even once we have returned back home in the afterlife.

I once had a personal question on my mind, and I decided to simply throw it out there and see what kind of response I got. My question was straightforward and blunt. *Do we still make love once we die?* Most people will be happy to know that the answer I received was yes. That opened up another question for me. *But how?* I already knew that we do not have the same physical make up in our new bodies. The answer was simple: We embrace each other in a hug, experiencing love like we have never experienced it before.

This answer was shown to me during another reading when a young man wanted to hold his girlfriend one last time using me (a bit like the film, *Ghost*). When I looked at my arms with my physical eyes, I didn't look any different. But when I used my spirit eyes, I looked different and *felt* like a man. The muscles in my arms felt much larger and more defined. When he hugged her through me, she felt the same as I did. We were able to feel the true depth of the love flowing through our bodies without any barriers in the way. It was a mind blowing experience—one I have not had again. So, answers come in many ways . . .

You may ask why ask such a question? Well, we all love a hug and the experience of a loving relationship. I thought one day, *What would I miss here when I go back home to the afterlife?* I wondered what happened when we meet up with our loved ones again. I was more than pleased with the answer I received. If you have any questions, always speak up and ask them. Be inquisitive and keep an open mind. Doing so opens up a much bigger world in which we live and share with people living here now and who have returned back home.

∞

TEN

Light at the End of the Tunnel

Movies, books, folklore, legends . . . We've all heard references to "the light at the end of the tunnel." Well, I hate to be the bearer of bad news but guess what? There isn't an actual tunnel. Instead, this so-called "tunnel" is an internal reflection of experiences from our lives. We hear in near-death experiences that some folks pass through a tunnel and reach a great light at the end of it. They believe that the light at the end of the tunnel is heaven—an actual place. They think that the light tells them they have officially reached heaven. Again, I hate to say this but no, that is not so.

Stand still and look at yourself in the mirror. After you've taken a good look, step back and take a look at the world around you. Congratulations! You have found the kingdom of heaven. *Huh? What is she talking about?* you wonder. *I'm already in heaven?* You may not believe me now, but you will one day. Let me try to explain.

Our loved ones in the afterlife live around us in the many rooms of the earth. Earth is a room, so to speak, that is part of what is called and referred to as heaven. We do not have to die to reach it because, as I just said, we are already in it. Furthermore, this is why we have a sixth sense, or an attunement in which we can communicate with everyone in life. Generally speaking, life is the kingdom of heaven.

The only reason we do not see earth as the kingdom of heaven is because of the many different levels of experiences that are constantly going on. Some are categorized as good and some are considered bad. But these are all labels that have very little meaning. Our physical eyes limit us to only seeing a small piece of the whole. We assume the little piece we hold is the whole. However, this small piece is part of a bigger picture, which is part of an even bigger picture—one so enormous that it is never fully explored because it never ends and it never began. Life does not stop feeling a new creation, and this is why the picture never stops growing.

Think about it for a moment. Think about how small we truly are in the grand scheme of things. Imagine that tiny piece you hold inside of you, or the little shadow that you encase yourself in. How does it compare to the size of the entire world? It's almost impossible to even wrap our minds around the concept. This is why we move into our next afterlife bodies so we can see more than what our physical bodies led us to believe. And even then, this all depends on our free will and choice. Remember, if life reflects something we do not like, we have the power inside of us to change the reflections and the experiences we wish to have.

The truth is and always has been amongst the stillness of the stream. It is in the nothingness of waiting for the seasons to change. It is in the blades of grass that grow and in everything around us and in us. We hold the secret of the light, and that secret is life. In fact, we are our own lights. Most of us just don't realize that until we cross over to the other side of the fence.

Yes, this truth suddenly comes to everyone at the time of when we let go of our physical bodies. Our vehicles crumble back to earth while the secrets of life are revealed to us. The light we see at the end of the tunnel is, in fact, *us*. The light is our own light and power of us shining right back at us. It is a place from within that has always been there, waiting.

On the other hand, we may hear about entering darkness at the moment of letting go of our physical bodies. This is where the shadows of earth and what we believe is still our truth lie. We see what we believe. Yet, when we are ready—be it while on earth or in the afterlife of life—our brightest light will be seen. It will shine amongst the many lights of lives and help guide us. Our internal light is the real us. It is the essence of us—the *feeling* of us.

We should take advantage of enjoying heaven on earth while we're here. If we cannot quite see it yet, it is because we are not thinking with an open mind. Our experiences are blanketing who we are, which in turn blocks the reflection of who we are. But we will never lose ourselves if we have faith. The great secret of our light is to simply be aware of what we believe. Remember, what we believe reflects straight back at us.

If we do not like what we see when we look at ourselves or at the world, we need to go ahead and make changes to our lives. If we change what we believe, we will change what we experience. We give ourselves our own restrictions. No one else can keep us from changing for the better unless we give them the power to do so. Our keys of freedom are the free choice that we will always have. We will always be free unless we believe that we are not. Again, the choice is ours.

What we see in the mirror today is not who we really are. That is just a reflection of what we believe at that moment in time—a reflection of the kingdom of heaven we are currently creating and experiencing. No one can force us into anything that we have not already agreed to. We need to realize how powerful we are. We need to follow our light—working it, being it, and creating it. Our light is who we are, not the physical bodies we oftentimes believe we are trapped in. The real us shines for all to see even when the clouds and the storms block out the sun. Our true reflections are always there if we believe and want to see them strongly enough.

∞

ELEVEN

What is Reflection?

Mirror, mirror, on the wall . . . who is the fairest of them all? *Smash!* Oh, no! Supposedly, a cracked mirror brings us seven years of bad luck. Regardless of if that's true or not, I was always fascinated by mirrors as I was growing up. *Do mirrors have a voice?* I often wondered. How strange it would be if they could talk. I am sure they would have a million-and-one stories to tell . . .

When I was living at the children's home, I would look at the mirror and talk to it whenever I was feeling sad. Sometimes I would even cry to it. Silly as it sounds, to me, the mirror was a portal to where my mother and father were. At the time, I wasn't sure where death had taken them to. I figured that looking and talking to them through old photographs of them or through the mirror was my way of reconnecting with them. Crying to the mirror was safe. I knew it wouldn't shout, laugh, judge, or abandon me. Above all, I knew it wouldn't reject me. In fact, I felt safe with the mirror when it was just us. (But I was always slightly on edge whenever I talked to it. I was nervous someone would catch me and label me as even more of an outcast.)

Later, I discovered how much I loved music. I would have some music on from some old film and start singing along and dancing to it all while in front of the mirror. During those few moments, I would escape my sad world and travel through my dreams into the world of that particular film. The music would take me to a place I would rather be—anywhere than in the children's home. I took myself to a place that was full of smiles and happiness from the heart. It was an enchanted place where dreams come from. It was much better than my lonely reality.

Because I had such a difficult time relating to people after the negative experiences I had been through growing up, I became lost in the fantasy world. I turned into a film fanatic, watching the happily-ever-after endings over and over. I saw how marriage apparently made everything okay. I decided that I wanted a happy ending to *my* story, too. But I was in for a big shock, not knowing much about life outside of the foster care system.

In foster care, we were kept away from life, functioning in our little box of our children's home. A bunch of us shared the same bedroom. We never went to the shops to buy clothes or shoes. Instead, there was a big cupboard on the landing at the top of the stairs. Whatever fit us from that cupboard was what we wore; we didn't knowing anything different than this. If we had pocket money (which was rare), we used it to buy penny sweets. Oh, what a delight that was!

In the summertime, we would take art lessons in the hall and go to Saturday morning pictures. These fun activities were held for children in foster care. All the same faces from our institutional community would be there, but our faces would be locked in our own ways—blank, for the most part. We did not really look at people from the outside world. Most outsiders didn't want to mix with people like us. Our world and our reflections of ourselves were completely skewed. Where we lived was nowhere near what a "normal" home was like, but the children's home was home to us. It was all we knew. Sometimes, people at school would ask me what it's like not having a mother and father. I would shrug and ask them what it's like having them.

Many of my childhood experiences would remind me that I was an orphan and always would be. When I was around the age of seven, there was a gymnastics performance at school one evening; students were supposed to present their gymnastics skills to all the parents. I walked to the school with my little gym bag, put on my leotard, and waited with all my classmates until it was our time to do our performance. I took my place on the mat and did a handstand and a one-handed cartwheel. Everyone smiled and clapped. I sat back down and smiled, too; I had never done a one-handed cartwheel before.

At the end of the performances, the parents cheered for their children. All of my classmates ran over to their respective mothers and fathers for hugs and lots of praise. I suddenly felt sad as I stood there, alone. I hesitated, unsure whether I should just leave or pretend I was waiting for my parents to walk over to me. My head bowed in shame. I was so different from the other kids without my mother and father there—without having parents at all. I watched from the corner of my eye as mothers helped their kids get dressed. Fathers were all smiles as they showered their kids with hugs. Watching all of this made me realize how much I missed out on by not having my parents anymore. I quickly got dressed and left the gym. No one noticed me leave.

It doesn't matter, I reminded myself as I headed back to the children's home. *Today, I noticed me. I smiled for me with my one-*

handed display. I showed up at the event to see me. I had to remind myself to stay positive often at the children's home. I was the only one who was an orphan there. All the kids still had parents; they just all had problems. They still had grandparents to spoil them. They could say they had families. I belonged to the children's home, being passed from one staff member to the next whenever it was closed for the holidays. I was lucky that they would take me in during those times out of the kindness of their hearts. These mini vacations gave me a glimpse of a real family home—so different from anything I had ever known.

As I gained new experiences, I realized that no one was like me. I felt like an alien as the world stared back at me, judging me. I finally accepted the fact that I was different and always would be. And sadly, I learned and saw firsthand how the world treats people who are different. I wanted to explain to people that they just didn't know me and that's why they couldn't understand me. Instead, they chose to keep their distance. People don't want to take the time to understand what they don't know. They don't want to deal with those who are damaged. But how can we understand something if we have never experienced it? This is something we can't learn from a book. Getting others to understand and accept people who are "different" soon became my battle later on.

When I was sixteen years old, my social worker suggested that I create a family scrapbook to try and piece my family tree together. I did not want to go there at all. My childhood had done nothing for me. Its reflection, I remember, only caused me pain. I did not want to revisit the pains of hell that I had buried deep down so well. I didn't want to suddenly attempt to resurrect all the secrets that had been forced upon me.

In pain, I didn't know what else to do but to run away. I found my niece of my real family—my real sister's daughter. She took me in. She phoned the foster family where I had been placed to let everyone know I was okay. And although my niece's hands were tied, she knew the pain I felt. It was comforting to finally be with someone who could relate to what I had been going through. Those few days were precious. She told me about my parents. I told her how I have the ability to see dead people. I was nervous at the response I would get after sharing that information. But I was surprised at her reply.

She smiled and told me that my grandmother had been able to see dead people, too. She used to read tea leaves and talk to the dead through a photograph. They would talk back to her. At last, I found someone in my family who was like me! Overcome with emotions, I opened up to my niece, admitting to her how much I hated my life. I pleaded with her to help me. She listened to me for a long time, but then told me she could not help because the law said I needed to stay in foster care until I reached the age of eighteen.

It all felt like a prison sentence. My crime was that my parents died and left me behind; somehow, it was my fault. This self-loathing slowly morphed into a reflection that I hated as the years passed. I was depressed with it all; it consumed me. I had two more years to go before I reached eighteen, but that seemed like an eternity. I desperately wanted to be with my parents. I was tired of being lost and alone. I hated being shuffled in and out of various foster homes, having to adapt to new people and ways of doing things each time I went somewhere different.

One clear vision I remember was visiting day. All of the children would stand in a line in the lounge, waiting for the new foster people to come. They would walk up and down, looking at us . . . judging us. They would engage us in small talk, but that was about it. When the visiting time was up, we would go outside to play. It was simple as that. Once again, we'd be back to the familiar life we had, that is, until one of the children's home staff members pulled one of us aside to say that new people wanted to take us out for the day . . .

I was picked for a particular family. The parents already had two boys and a girl, but their little girl was very shy. They figured she needed a sister to play with; maybe a sister would help her come out of her shell. Little did they know, I was the complete opposite of their daughter. I was an outspoken girl who wasn't afraid to speak my mind. I never had anything to lose otherwise.

As soon as I moved in with my new family, I quickly realized that I could not be me. For starters, I had jumped into a middle class family—a family who didn't have the same roots as my own family. This family's reflection was not the same as mine; they had never shared any similar experiences. On one occasion, I put my bread into my hand and started to butter it with the other, the same way I always had. I was scolded for buttering my bread that way. "Use the plate and not your hand!" the mother said sternly. I nodded, remembering to use a plate next time.

They also wanted me to learn how to play the piano. I hated this, too, because my hands were so small. It was practically impossible to move them over the keys properly. But I had to at least try to change for this family so that I could fit in to their family plans. I had to make sure I looked good with them. They thought it was important to impress the community and the church congregation. And I was pretty good at blending in, for the most part. Yet, behind closed doors, my new parents hugged and praised my brothers and sister. I, on the other hand, received no hugs from them. This behavior confused me. Was I not good enough?

I thought families were supposed to be close with lots of hugs, casual talking, and laughter. This family was like a regiment with rules, regulations, and lists of what to do. They seemed entirely different from when we had first met. In fact, we began having many arguments, day in and day out. I was fighting for me—that little piece of me. It was all that I had left from my family who had died and left me alone. No matter what, I would not let my new family take the rest of me. I held my breath, bit my tongue, and attempted to fit in the best I could.

In the end, though, my placement didn't work out. The daughter was jealous of me, and we clashed in too many ways. Our paths split up for the rest of our lives. In retrospect, I now know that it didn't work because the family's expectations were much different than my own. They thought they could have me and mold me into their perfect daughter who would help their other daughter come out of her cocoon. I simply wanted folks to love me for me. Metaphorically speaking, they had judged me only by my cover had I been a book. They didn't take into account my contents, my depth. They never got to know me for who I was. They only saw what they *wanted* to see.

I did not fulfill their wish of having the perfect daughter; I could not be what they wanted me to be. It is strange how reflections always show up in the end—the hidden truths. Either way, I thanked the family for doing their best with what they had to work with. I had taught myself at an early age to not hold my expectations of others too high, and so I wasn't too overly upset by the falling out. At the same time, I thanked myself for staying true to myself. I wasn't a bad person when I lived with the family. In fact, I left them with happy memories. I just wasn't a good fit with them.

A reflection may be made of many personalities—another tongue in the language of life, so to speak. We all have our own books of experiences. These books may share many different pages with other people, but we're not always going to be on the same page. Have you ever had a conversation with someone where you think you're both talking about the same thing but then suddenly realize you're both lost and confused with what the other person is saying? Again, you're reading from the same book but you're simply on different pages. That's another example of how easy miscommunication can be.

Miscommunication happens when someone is absorbed in his or her life and does not have much time or energy to pay attention to anything else. We can easily become self-absorbed. It happens all the time. Conversations we may engage in are from inside our own boxes. Simply put, if we don't stop what we're doing and truly focus on what other people are saying, their messages are going to get lost in translation. Our communication will more than likely hit a brick wall and no messages from either side will be understood. Again, this leads to frustration, which can lead to arguments. It is so *easy* to avoid confrontation or petty fighting if we just step out of our own little words for a while and pay attention to what other people have to say.

When I was growing up, I was often reprimanded for thinking too much. I analyzed too much. I came across as too intense. Hearing these words from many different people—some who I had just met—made me self-conscious. I began wondering if people were always saying negative things about me. I mean, I was already considered an alien by people I had told about my gift. Now I was a weirdo, too? Why? How come people were criticizing me for working out experiences in my head? It had always been difficult for me to understand most people because their reflections hardly ever matched their words. Their actions and body language did not match up with their hopes, wishes, and dreams. And *I* was the strange one? At least I always put it all out there.

But instead of getting upset, I simply thanked everyone for noticing this personality trait about me—for highlighting it. Because of that, I became highly aware of my mind, my actions, my body language—my whole package. And whenever I would find myself thinking negative thoughts or feeling down about my life, I would hold my head up a little higher and thank myself for carrying on being me. I would never pretend to be someone who I wasn't. I was and continue to be a deep thinker, an analyzer. And I don't see anything wrong with that. Had I not carried on being me, I would not have been able to put together all the jigsaw pieces that helped explain all of the confusing experiences from my past. Being me—someone who pays extra close attention to details and signs—has allowed me to be excellent in my field of work, too.

I am labeled as "different" because I chose to embrace and learn a complicated language—one of silent thought, mind, and subtle actions that do not mirror the main reflection of a person. It takes a lot of piecing together of clues and information to get to the bottom of a meaning so that an experience makes sense to us. It all takes time and effort.

This also means sometimes visiting the darkest places inside ourselves—places we may spend a lifetime running away from. But facing the reflection of fear makes us stronger individuals in the end. Fear is only a reflection of the mind. It is not solid, like bumping into a table, for example. It's as real as what we think it and believe it to be. Fear is nothing without our will to feed it. If we simply stop feeding it, it will eventually go away.

Fear is a reflection of what is not understood. It comes from guesswork. Think of these sayings: *Mind your own business. Mind your back. Don't play mind games. It's a mind-numbing experience.* All of these words start with mind. Unfortunately, very little is understood about the mind. We are not taught how to use it, only how to *do* things. The "being" part is what confuses the reflection of "doing."

So, there is the *doing* reflection (physical body on earth, materialism, etc.). Doing symbolizes actions, which actually do not speak louder than words. There is also the *being* reflection (afterlife body, the real us, etc.). This symbolizes our feelings, or our essence. Doing and being are just two facets of reflections. If you think about it, when a baby is first born, what kinds of questions do we ask first? *How much does he or she weigh? What color hair or eyes does he or she have?* These are basic questions about the front cover of doing—the physical. We hardly ever ask how a baby is *being*. That would be an example of the afterlife reflection.

In our physical bodies, we are taught to focus on the doing of physical activities. We are taught to talk and do actions, such as walking or playing with toys, but no one teaches us the meanings behind any of these things. We only learn about the reflections of the many physical things that we use. When we get older, we buy electrical gadgets that are also not ruled by the mind; they are physically outside of ourselves. Luckily, these things come with instructions that show us how to work them properly. Yet, sometimes these pieces of paper or forms that we have to read or fill in scare us. Some people can follow instructions better than others. It all depends on how simple the instructions are and how they reflect back to our minds.

As you started to read this chapter on reflection, you probably read the title and took it for face value; the chapter would be all about looking at what's in front of us. Well, it is actually about looking *beyond* what we see at first glance—what we see with our physical eyes. It is about the real reflection of feelings and essence that reflect from all the physical doing words, thoughts, actions, and deeds.

Here, in the physical world, I will always be judged. Remarks will always be made about me behind my back, or in some cases, to my face. People will believe what they want to believe, and that's entirely okay. When things get too overwhelming at times, people have a tendency to become even more close-minded. They don't want to accept the truth—or they don't know how to. But in the adult mix of life—in a world that does not make much sense to anyone—my answer to the skeptical folks is this: *You just gotta laugh sometimes, right?* That's all any of us can really do.

Giggling has always managed to get me into a lot of trouble. My childlike spirit often acts like a child, finding things funny that children find funny. Adults will glare in my direction. Even my kids sometimes say, "Stop it, Mom! Act your age! You're not a kid anymore!"

Yes, that's true. I'm not a kid anymore. But I'm afraid my spirit will remain kidlike forever. I am who I am and I wear many coats in the reflection of my adult life. I have a mommy coat that helps me to be sensible and to love and care for my children. I wear my mommy coat when I cook, clean, and wash up around the house. I have a sensitivity coat for when I need to soothe any of my children's pain or when I need to be there for them in times of need. I have my professional coat for when I'm studying or doing readings for others. I also have my creative coat for when I participate in my dance class. Even though I have so many various coats for the different layers of my life, the underlying layer makes me *me*. And no matter how much I cover up the real me at times, my childlike spirit will always be there, ready to laugh and be silly. I can't hide who I truly am from myself.

Laughter is life. Being able to laugh and smile brings everything back into reality and puts it all in perspective for us. Our memories may serve us well for a while, but what is really learned and taken in when all is said and done? This is reflected by how much we know and by how well we treat others. No matter what coats we choose to wear in our lifetimes, we all move on the same as we came. We are all the same regardless of our experiences. No coat or armor will hide ourselves from who we really are. The self catches up with itself when it comes time to transition over to the afterlife. This is why we see older people owning up to past experiences they have had.

For example, a man in his seventies decides he now wants to admit wrong in something he did dozens of years ago. Why? Why does it even matter at this point? As we get older and nearer to moving on, we know we have to leave our physical lives and whatever baggage we may have accumulated behind—all the games that we may have played. Our materialistic toys and our looks of perfection are unnecessary in the afterlife. But we enter our consciousness of who we really are and know we have to face what belongs to us. *That* is what we decide is most important to us. We want to cross over to the other side of the fence with clear minds and open hearts. We don't want to feel mentally punished or shamed.

All of our experiences are records in our souls. What we deny only hurts us. The stretched elastic years of life all come pinging back when we enter the afterlife. All the pieces to our physical lives, if not faced before we cross over, go into our metaphorical backpacks, weighing us down and holding us back. Pain is only felt by the person who created it. If anyone tries to harm you in any way while in your physical body, remember that your body will reflect that pain back to the other person's soul when it's time for that person to enter the afterlife. There is such a thing as karma.

Oh, yes. *Everything* is noticed; no one can hide when it comes to committing acts of evil. It is part of the full story of life. We all fight for justice when we're living in our physical bodies. We forget the full picture of life. Remember, we sow what we reap. What we do to others will eventually reflect back on us. In the afterlife, no justice needs to be found. No fighting needs to take place. The laws of life stand strong. Rest assured, any unfinished business gets finished in the afterlife.

All life's gifts that surround us in our physical lives are tools to remind us of the laws of life—no judgment and no punishment outside of ourselves. What we choose to create will equally be our reflection to feel. Forgiveness is the biggest key. Any form of fighting on any level would become a war that no one would ever win. Whatever your part was in the fighting will come back for you to feel another day. People only see a reflection of their physical lives from this side of the fence.

We may *think* that some people get away with murder, but no one ever does. First of all, no one can murder another; they only destroy the physical body vehicle ahead of time. Remember, real life is eternity, and death is often confused for the end. Life is a continuation, and therefore murder is false. It is not real. In fact, it is a waste of time. People who attempt to murder others never actually kill *them*.

As I've mentioned, whatever is done is relived and felt. For example, someone *thinks* he or she has killed another person. When it comes time to transition to the afterworld, the killer will own the experience; that's who it belongs to. That person has made an agreement to share this experience in order to teach everyone else the truth, by example. The person who killed then feels everything that the person who was killed felt when the experience happened. The experience is relived in the shoes of the person who committed the crime, but from the victim's standpoint. The person who was murdered gets on with new experiences, free from feeling any of the past. However, that person has learned a lesson: Life is never in the hands of another person.

No one has the power to kill another, regardless of any side of the fence. Murderers are just fooled into thinking and believing that they have the ability to do so by the physical reflections of what they see. It is only the doer that believes this, not the receiver. Life goes on no matter what. This is why people from the afterlife are able to retell their experiences that they had while on earth. It does not matter how the physical body transitioned into the afterlife body, be it naturally in their sleep, an accident, or murder. These ways are all just labels to reflect an experience on earth. Everyone continues on and has a life story to tell.

People can judge, fight, or do anything they want to do. They are only playing their own game. They aren't playing with the whole game of life. A reflection has many meanings, layers, and facets. Each reflection has the ability to tell many life story experiences, all of which cannot harm or touch real life. We are constantly playing games of reflection with ourselves, similar to a fun house of mirrors, realizing how little we really know and understand about the world in which we live. But life has taken care of everything for us. Nothing is ever wasted. Nothing is ever hidden. Lessons are constantly being learned. Yes, life is ours for all of us to see and experience as we wish.

What kind of reflection do you see when you look in your mirror? I will leave this up to you to decide . . .

∞

TWELVE

Dodging the Bullet

Forrest Gump said, "Life is like a box of chocolates; you never know what you're gonna get." I couldn't have said it better myself. Like a box of chocolates, we are presented with so many opportunities in life. These opportunities lead to our various experiences. But what happens when we act on an opportunity and hate that experience? It's kind of like choosing a chocolate, biting into it, and realizing we hate the inside filling. Do we eat it all up quickly . . . or spit it out? Do we immediately learn from our mistakes . . . or do we keep tempting fate?

With chocolate, we can remember the shape or the taste of the bad ones and never eat them again. If we do choose to swallow the whole thing, it's only a moment of nastiness—and then it's gone. If only life's experiences were so easy and quick. Unfortunately, even our memories forget what they already know. It's a bit like being pregnant for the first time. The experience, itself, is overwhelming. It consumes the whole body from conception up until the birth. While it is often a painful experience for a woman to go through, the physical body has a clever way of deleting—or at least numbing—the actual painful parts. Children probably wouldn't have as many brothers and sisters if the pain was memorable! It seems like we all have selective memory from time to time.

As kids, we are constantly being told to eat our vegetables. Our parents smile and say our greens will make us big and strong. They say that eating our carrots will help us to see better. If we don't go to sleep early, the tooth fairy won't come and put money under our pillows. If we aren't good all year, Santa Claus won't come down the chimney. I could go on and on with these lines—and we always believed them.

We live in a world of fantasy—a world full of sayings that we practice and preach to our children after growing up and learning them ourselves. Ultimately, we follow the trail of make believe. In a way, we are built up to believe it's all true. If we look around at everything in life, we can clearly see that most of it is fabricated. Everyone seems to take part in this fantasy of life. And the strange thing is, this is what we see as *real*.

Our make believe outlook comes from an old lost truth that man has forgotten. It is a truth that isn't understood anymore. This lost truth is . . . *magic*. I'm not talking about card tricks or white rabbits in black top hats. I'm not talking about witches who come out in scores on Halloween night, the Easter bunny, or the tooth fairy and her magic fairy dust. I'm talking about bits and pieces of a truth being retold as make believe stories for us all to engage in. These stories allow us to create new traditions with our families and have certain holidays to keep the fantasy business alive. Even the fantasy has turned into fantasy money, too. We definitely fall for the commercialization of it all.

I am not a killjoy. In fact, I take part in a lot of these traditions, too—for the kids. These days, children see nice presents under the tree and beautifully decorated Easter eggs to eat or hide. They get to dress up as whatever they want to be for Halloween. But now, when they lose a tooth, they don't get as excited anymore for the tooth fairy. "Um, Mom? I'll just have the money instead of putting my tooth under my pillow. I am not five years old anymore; I know what really goes on . . ." they say. Sadly, the fantasy and its meaning are now lost, too, amongst the pretty packages and sacks of candy. They don't care about the history of these holidays. They just want their goods.

Our children are taught, early on, about believing in stories. Santa Claus is *real*. The Easter bunny is *real*. The tooth fairy is *real*. But all too quickly they have to adjust to the reality that we live in a world of make believe. It is such a letdown when they find out the facts. Why would our loved ones lie to us in the first place? We start living in a world of fantasy with so much to see and imagine, but suddenly, the show is over. There is nothing to see anymore.

It is all just an adult trap to keep our attention when we are children. These stories are told to cover up the adult world. The adult world is dull and boring. There are no magic wands to play with. Instead, there are just bills and piled up debt to deal with. But as kids, we forgot this sad truth. We get on the train of make believe and enter the world like the generations before. We play the same games all over again. We get to participate in the magic that time has forgotten. And deep down, we know that one day our kids will know these secrets. We silently hope that their friends will break the news because we don't want to break their hearts.

LOADED FANTASY GUN

I remember being at the playground as a little girl and sharing information about my life with another little girl. She shared personal information about herself, and soon we became close friends. I knew I could trust her in ways I hadn't ever been able to trust others before. When I was around my new best friend, I felt a truth deep inside. I realized that children *do* understand and care for each other. Or at least they do before the battles and games are later played as they grow up.

These games tend to start when we enter high school. We become competitive, selfish, and jealous of each other. Fighting and talking badly about the other person replaces the love and caring we used to share. In fact, it seems that we stop understanding each other altogether almost overnight. Our priorities change. *We* change. But even though I started middle school without being as close to my elementary school best friend as I had been, I carried with me the positive feelings and traits of a good friend as I entered the next phase of my life.

In high school, I eventually found a new best friend. Together, we attempted to make it through feelings of confused despair. We were living in a world of fighting—a war that seemed to have no end. But this war was amongst peers, and bullets came from the mouth. We figured our best option was to get away from everything. Oftentimes, we'd run away only to be found by the police again.

Ultimately, I tried escaping because I was so unhappy with being in foster care. My friend was also depressed that her family was breaking in two. We met in the middle of all the sadness and negativity, desperately trying to find love in our empty lives. Naturally, we made many mistakes as we attempted to navigate through the adult world without any mentors. All we wanted was to feel loved. Instead, we walked through our teenage years with thorns in our sides—aching pain that became etched into our bodies and souls with every move we made. And while our pain was not seen by the adults we encountered, our actions definitely got noticed. As I've said before, actions don't speak louder than words. Our actions only spoke a language that we understood.

These two childhood friends were two girls I trusted my life with. They didn't judge me. They understood the real me. How were we able to form such close bonds despite our negative upbringings? It's because what we saw in each other was the same as what we saw in ourselves. Even though we were on different pages of our lives, we were reading, so to speak, from a similar book. We were able to really connect with each other. We mirrored and recognized our similar language of pain. We immediately understood and accepted each other for who we really were. There was no game playing.

I graduated from high school with the help of my small safety net of friends. Even though my life experiences seemed to alienate me from everyone I came in contact with, these friends helped me survive the toughest years of my life. Not only did I leave high school with a flimsy diploma, I left with a better sense of who I was and who I wanted to eventually become. My experiences were helping to shape me.

At sixteen, I found a job caring for the elderly. But I quickly realized how difficult the job was. It didn't sit right with me. I didn't like what I saw whenever I was there. The elderly were treated as old, worn out flesh and nothing more. When I saw what was going on, I complained to the management, trying to stand up for the elderly people's rights, but that didn't get me anywhere. I insisted the folks should be treated with the utmost care and respect—like regular human beings. It was not okay for staff members to lose their tempers and push them about. But my protests were useless. I could not work for such a cruel system and decided it would be in my best interest to leave after only a year.

Around the same time, I got into my first close relationship. Suddenly, I was experiencing a new language of body and mind.

This language became another kind of fantasy tool—a weapon of mind games. At first I felt safe around this guy; I trusted him. But then warning signs began to pop up. He began trying to control me with his abusive words. And sadly, I let him. I was blind and desperate to be loved. But this was false love. I believed I had found what I had been searching for so many years. I mean, this guy paid attention to me! He didn't push me away. Even though he put me down with his words, it was better than everything I had experienced in the past. I figured that's what real love was.

I had become an easy target for him. My honesty was my crime. Whenever he got upset, it was always my fault. I believed him, having heard this for most of my life—the groove of this record so deep in my mind. Slowly, I could feel the real me slipping away as I stayed in our relationship. I was torn. Part of me began to realize that what we had wasn't love. Deep down, I knew love wasn't supposed to hurt so much. But the other part of me was afraid to be alone again. I argued back and forth with myself for a long time before I decided I had to do what was best for me.

One day, I mustered up the courage to break free from him. The relationship wasn't benefiting either of us; it hadn't been for a while. I got out of his car and took a deep breath before speaking. I felt detached from my words as I told him that I didn't want to go out with him anymore. Then I shut the door, not looking back. I focused on walking to the freedom of my front door and cracked a small smile. *I still see me*, I thought. *I will be okay*. I still had a life in front of me. The possibilities were endless. I still had the chance to find happiness.

"*What?* I got you out of the gutter and now you don't want to go out with me anymore!?" he screamed. His words hit me straight in my soul and stabbed at my heart. He thought I owed him for everything he had done for me. He knew all about my childhood past and was manipulating the break up to keep me chained to him. My story was now turning against me. He wanted to keep me locked up in a love that hurt both of us. Why?

My mind raced, unsure of what I should do. And while my mind urged me to keep walking toward my door, my heart couldn't let go of the love I wished we shared. *Maybe I can help him be a better boyfriend*, I reasoned, as I turned back toward his car. He was right; in a way, I owed him. I had come from the gutter. I should've been grateful that anyone would want to go out with me, right? In retrospect, I was so disillusioned by his constant negative words that I actually began to think there was truth in what he said.

We stayed in our destructive relationship. I always hoped he would change; he couldn't have cared less about treating me with kindness and true love. We stayed together for convenience. One day, we had a party to attend. It was my niece's birthday, as well as mine. We thought that a joint party with all of our friends would be fun. Drinking heavily was a "family" tradition. I knew it wouldn't be long before the alcohol would drown my depression, at least for a short while. Sure enough, I got so drunk that I blacked out.

Four weeks later, I realized I had missed my period. I headed straight for the clinic to take a pregnancy test. The technician said the results were negative. Four weeks after that, I missed my period again. I went back to the clinic, confused. My second pregnancy test results were the same: negative. *What is going on?* I wondered.

Two weeks after the negative tests, my boyfriend began to panic. He seemed more worried about the situation than I was. Determined to find out what was going on with my body, he took me to the clinic for a third test. The results come back positive. "What?" I cried. "How can this be? I already took two tests and you told me they were negative!" The technician calmly explained that those sorts of things can happen. She then told me that I was ten weeks pregnant. I would have two weeks to decide if I wanted to keep the baby or not. After twelve weeks, I wouldn't be able to have an abortion because the baby would've been too far developed by then.

Leaving the clinic, I held my tummy, thinking about the new life that was growing inside of me—a secret only my boyfriend and I knew. He told me there were no options; I had to get rid of it. I was still in foster care and his mother happened to be a foster parent. He was afraid that my pregnancy would get us into a lot of trouble. His words sunk in slowly. I didn't say how I felt. I was too scared; my hands felt like they were tied. Due to situation and circumstance, on one hand I had a new life inside of me. On the other, I would have to deal with Social Services and angry adults if I went through with the pregnancy. Was it worth it? *He's right,* I thought. *I'm just from the gutter . . .* I knew I had to get an abortion.

The cost was £350 pounds. Of course, being teenagers, that was a lot of money that we didn't have. My boyfriend decided to sell his entire record collection to get money. Each night, I cried before the dreaded day. I felt like I now had the label of "murderer" because of my decision. Or at least that's what the church and my foster family would think. *Great, can my life get any worse?* I wondered. I felt lost and lonely inside. And on the day of the abortion, my boyfriend handed me the money and dropped me off in front of the clinic. I couldn't wait for the next day when this problem would be gone. I bought a teddy bear for our unborn child. "Sorry . . ." I whispered as I walked inside, hoping the baby would understand why I couldn't go forward with the pregnancy.

No one knew about the abortion. It was a well hidden secret. By staying silent about the situation, I thought that everyone would stay safe; nothing would change. The days and weeks that followed, my boyfriend and I carried on as if nothing had happened. We decided it would be best if we never spoke of our secret ever again.

We arranged to get married because the ties had now been made. We shared a false love of situation and circumstance—a façade of love that was created the moment I turned back toward his car after attempting to leave him way back when. This love was not seen by us as equal. Instead, it was a love where he would always have the upper hand. I would always owe him. I was from the gutter. I wasn't recognized as a normal human being. I had no one in the world but him. Because of this, he had more power behind him for having a better start in life than me. This power would tower over me for the rest of our relationship.

It took me many years to fully understand how to dodge the bullets of hurtful words. For way too long, I believed that they had paralyzing power and control over me. It took a long time for me to realize that I was capable of making my own choices. I was responsible for finding my own happiness. And one day, with too many years of negative experiences built up inside, I finally found the courage to stand on my own two feet. It made me feel . . . alive.

I look back at everything with love in my heart, not hate. If I had not faced the opposite of what love is, I would never have recognized love when I finally understood it. The love I needed to find first was love for myself. The missing piece I had been trying so hard to find in the many people I met was actually in myself all along. I needed to accept myself for who I was; I needed to love me for me.

I had spent so many years searching for love outside of myself, desperately hoping that someone else would give it to me. I held on with all my might. I put up with the bits and pieces of love that I received, building them up to what I believed would make me feel whole. But I always wanted more than what I had. Deep down, I knew the love I had wasn't genuine. Rather than to admit defeat, I would compromise with myself in the search of happiness. I soon realized that one should never do that with oneself. By the time I reached thirty, I'd had enough. It dawned on me that if I wanted to change the pattern of my self-destructive ways and my complete unhappiness, I would have to change *me*.

I had been hit by so many bullets of this fantasy game for far too long. I now wanted the bullets to go away. These weapons start with the mind—for power and control—and take over people who don't know how to dodge the bullet. But what should we do if we are always in close firing range? Sometimes stepping out of the line of fire is easier said than done. I learned the hard way. I finally realized that I needed to *move* out the way before I got hit one too many times. I needed to remove myself from the hurtful situations. These harmful games can stop if we take the mind game toys away from those who are using them.

Wake up and recognize the game plan if you find yourself in a situation similar to what I was in. All the weapons that are used against us start with the mind to disable us. If this attack isn't enough to break us down, we are told that our lives are mapped out already. We are told what to wear, how to behave, who you see or who we can't, what money we can have, etc. It all starts with the purse strings of our youth when we are vulnerable and open to anything. This fantasy game of lying becomes a game in which the rules hold us back from being able to love ourselves.

I am not a murderer because I had had an abortion. The truth of life I have learned to see and acknowledge is the truth that our real bodies are more than just flesh and bones; our souls live for all eternity. In fact, I adore my afterlife children. They play around me in the kitchen or in the living room. They follow me and still grow up the same. They just don't need their vehicle bodies to exist. I still see my children as if they never left me.

Let's dodge the bullets if or when they fly in our direction. When hurtful people are ready to disarm their fantasy guns, they will see that the bullets they shot were actually all about them. Real love does not involve weapons. Let's learn from the bullets that we've taken in our lifetimes. Let's rise above our shooters and show them that we are better than what they think we are. We can make our own happiness without them.

I had touched upon magic earlier. Magic comes from inside all of us. True magic does not come from potions and spells. It comes from our free will. If it is not free, it is forced. We need to differentiate between the two and take action, if we have to, in order to create our own happiness. To make our internal magic work, we need to know our minds and use our free will. When we do that, our wishes will be our commands. If our wishes are not coming true for us, we need to find our own footing and take a leap of faith to start anew. We need to face forward and never look back. My biggest mistake was turning back around to face my boyfriend. I now have the tools to be happy. In fact, I had them all along.

Love is not owned, owed, or borrowed. It is free and what our free will wants for us. Remember to recognize the fantasy gun and dodge the bullets it may shoot. These bullets cannot harm us if we don't let them. We cannot believe that the gun is real and loaded. The choice is ours. If someone tries to play mind games with us, it means they have very little to offer.

It's what we feel on the inside that tells us what is real, especially when it comes to finding true love. If something is weighing on our minds morning, noon, and night, we are probably in the process of being hit by someone's fantasy bullets; we need to wake up and dodge the destruction. Our lives are in our own hands. We need to keep our minds when others try to manipulate them. Sometimes the simple act of observing what is really going on will let us really *see* what we need to do. Technically, we are already free—more than we will ever know while we reside in our physical bodies—but situations and circumstances often make us forget what we know. Only we can create our own happiness for ourselves.

∞

THIRTEEN

GUIDED AFTERLIFE TOUR—FAMILIES

We choose to become parts of the families in which we are born into when we decide to have another life experience on earth. We choose these families while we are at home in the afterlife. Basically, we sit down and think about who would benefit us the most for the experiences we want when we are on earth. We look for families who match not only our intentions, but the intentions of the family members who are already on earth, taking part in their own experiences. We decide if we want to become a part of those experiences.

Let's start at the basics. In the physical world, we grow inside the womb so that our bodies can mature and be ready for birth. We all know that we are surrounded by the amniotic sac of fluid when we are in the womb. No matter how many babies may be in the womb, they all have their own space for nine months. Being in such a small space, but in our *own* small space, enables the continuity of free will and choice—not separate or singular. This space also allows us to find ourselves amongst the crowds we share life with. We learn that no matter where we are in life in this world or the next, we always have our own space. Sometimes, space gets confused with place; these two words do not mean the same thing. Space is empty space filled with personal free will and choice that goes on to create experiences. Empty space contains everything. Personal space is always ours. We've heard the sayings, "daydreaming," "staring into space," and "looking at nothing," right? This space is our life force, or our safety net, while on earth—our connection back to the afterlife. The umbilical cord is symbolic of this connection. It is cut at birth, yet we have tiny scars to remember that it is still there.

Our belly buttons show us in a symbolic way. They show us the connection a baby has with its mother while in the womb, and spiritually it mirrors our connection back home in the afterlife. As I said before, the secrets of the universe and that of life are not really secrets at all. They are just interpreted that way so we take longer to remember what we are all about and where we came from. Life, from the beginning when we start in the womb, guides us to all the answers of life itself. Really, it is that simple.

The earth is a big mirror image and everything on it mirrors the truth. After all, we are born as babies for a reason: Life and all of its so-called secrets is so easy to comprehend that a baby knows and understands it. Babies are born with no speech or a language, right? Who teaches them how to communicate? Because of where babies come from—home in the afterlife—they do not need to talk to communicate. They feel and know it all instantly. The biggest shock to babies born on earth is why adults do not understand them. In fact, this is why they cry to get our attention. It's all they can do at first. From then on, everything is taught: how we speak, what language we speak, etc.

The space around us, be it noisy space or within the internal silence of ourselves, is governed by what we tune in to. It does not matter if we tune in to our own thoughts and fears or in to the people around us; we always have a connection within the self to the afterlife that we call home.

As we learn to use our new physical bodies, we gradually forget where we have come from. We join the flow of life and all its dictating and control. This helps us forget who we totally are and that we started life with everything we needed for our earthly experiences. We are born being equipped with just our physical vehicles and all our knowledge stored inside. We are able to connect with the afterlife whenever we need help, support, or guidance. We have a lifeline, or our own personal frequency and vibration to use whenever we so desire. This connection to the afterlife is very strong at the time of our birth. However, for some of us, as our physical experiences take over, this connection can become weak and lost amongst the flow of earthly dictation and expectations that are put on us. Most of us forget that we can find ourselves and our sense of purpose in our own personal space.

Sadly, this space becomes frightening to be in because when we enter this silence during quiet times with ourselves, we are frightened by the unknown. At times, we may become confused with the many different thoughts that we have—some from our minds and some that are gut feelings, or our instincts. But we always have the little voice of guidance from within. This is built in; it stays with us no matter what life experiences we may have on earth or in the afterlife. This is our connection that you can turn to or tune in to whenever we want.

As we already know, babies are born naked and with no use of language. They do not come with an instruction manual. Babies know they hold the truth of all life (which is simple, as you are learning) deep inside. The difference is that the physical body forgets it is the earthly life which makes remembering the truth complicated—and even more so as babies are taught different things by adults who have already completely forgotten the truth. Babies have their own maps, their own navigational systems, their own inner guidance, their own knowing, etc. All they need are clothes to keep them warm and food to help nourish and grow their earthly bodies. They also need knowledge about the physical world and how to use their new bodies to navigate around earth. Being taught a language helps them to communicate and properly express themselves while in their physical bodies.

It is when we suddenly remember parts of an experience that we already knew we had chosen—often referred to as déjà vu—do we also remember where we truly came from. These types of experiences put our afterlife bodies in sync with our physical mirrored body experiences. For an instance, they match each other and everything becomes clear. We feel as if we have already experienced something—every single detail of that moment. In a way, we have. Our afterlife bodies chose these moments, watched them on film, so to speak, and mapped out the life experiences for us to have while on earth before we chose to play them out for ourselves in the physical way with our physical bodies. It is comparable to watching a film, like *Avatar*, and then wishing to experience that role on earth. The only difference is that we have the maps inside of us already. By the time we have gotten used to our new physical bodies, the materialistic life experiences going on around us by other people doing the same types of things encourage us to forget why we came back in the first place.

We waste most of our physical lives trying to remember. You are probably familiar with the phrase, "Go away and find yourself. Don't come back until you have." Some folks lose their way for a bit, so they go back home to the afterlife with their life maps still inside them. In fact, they have not even looked at them. But they get back home and everything is shown on "film" back to them—the lives they had planned in the first place to experience. They are also shown the films of the experiences they actually had while back on earth. Both films are compared to each other, and the afterlife people then tend to laugh about what happened. It's like being blindfolded halfway through the earthly life experience and trying to remember what you knew when you could see, spending most of your time trying to maneuver around without sight. Others remember earlier on or they don't forget their roots so easily.

WHERE WE LIVE

Where we choose to live is only useful to us in the same ways that aid our physical bodies in keeping warm, staying healthy, etc. In fact, anything more than this is not considered a bonus to the real us. The buildings we live in are all different—many different shapes and sizes. These places are simply mirror images of our real homes. They show and signify the many rooms that there are in the big afterlife home (which, if you remember, houses all of us under one roof).

In the afterlife, there are no barriers or walls; everything is seen and available. But we still have privacy because this falls under respect, free will, and choice. Privacy is something that is not infringed upon. There are only simple rules: respect, truth, knowing, naked truth (not to be confused with standing naked with no clothes on). Everything is for everyone, and there is no fear or threat anywhere. How is this possible? While everyone has everything, no one owns anything. Let me explain.

On earth, we think there is limited availability of almost everything—only enough to go around for some people for so long. The only problems that occur in acquiring things on earth include how they are controlled, how available they are, and how they are shared. But there is always plenty to go around—more than enough to go around for all eternity. There is no such thing as lack of anything, and we know this truth back home in the afterlife. However, the controllers and dictators do not want us to remember that. Instead, they want us to believe that resources are sparce. They want us to believe their game of make believe so that they can appear more powerful than us. Our free will and choice are more powerful than them though. So should we listen to the illusions or start to remember and listen to ourselves? This choice is for us to make and only us. No one else can hold the keys to our freedom.

Our houses mirror the many rooms of life in its totality under one roof—a *massive* home that houses all that is with its many (open) floors and levels. Think of all of us as one big family who can explore all that life has to offer together. We are able to experience the many layers of life's experience no matter what side of the fence we're on. Remember, we are all the same underneath when we are born and when we strip the various layers away. If we take away our materialistic possessions, and we take away our physical bodies, what are we left with? We're left with ourselves and all of our experiences. We have our unique essence and all that we are—the same as when we were in the afterlife. Only now, we have more experiences in tow from the journeys we took using our physical bodies on earth.

The house has two pillars that hold up a building at the front. These pillars mirror our personal space. They give us room to breathe, observe, see, and explore. Space is our magic and where magic comes from. But why are we encouraged to be scared of silence and space, stillness and nothingness? It's because we often lose the connection of our roots—our true source. We also lose that pinch of magic, our free will and choice—our essence. These sacred items make up our keys to our freedom. They rest silently and safely until we notice where they are—where they've been all along.

But one thing is for sure: No one can take our keys of freedom away from us no matter how powerful they think they are. Our personal keys unlock the many life experiences that we have under the one giant roof of home in the afterlife. Our keys all lead back to the same gate. They are us, in us, and who we are and are all about. We have the ability to unlock what we want to achieve and experience. We can take advantage of this opportunity if we remember to find ourselves in this busy world. After all, we are born with our keys and precious maps so that we can explore as many rooms as we like on earth the same way we explore back home. In the end, it all comes back to the self.

∞

FOURTEEN

Guided Afterlife Tour—Knowledge, Wisdom, and Language versus Telepathy

Our physical bodies grow up fast. In what seems like no time at all, we can walk, feed ourselves, communicate, and do many other things, like explore our surroundings. We start to venture out into the big wide world, realizing there are so many new things to see, taste, and feel. We experience a world still innocent through our eyes when we are children. That is, until the experiences that build up in our internal memory albums begin to tell us otherwise.

Most of us have seen children throw themselves on the floor because they are very frustrated and cross. More often than not, they act this way because they are confused. This behavior does not initially come from their minds. It is just transferred from their afterlife bodies as soul memories and expressed via the physical brain. You see, in the afterlife, what we feel and express is instant, without any gaps. For example, if we are used to turning our TVs on with a remote control, but then we go to live somewhere different where we suddenly have to get up and walk over to the TV every time we want to turn it on, the process of turning on the TV becomes much slower. It's not what we're used to back home. We'd probably get fed up fast knowing we used to have an easier way of turning on the TV.

Sometimes doing things differently makes us feel like we are going backwards. This is why young children often find it hard to explain what they mean and feel. They are used to thinking something and the people with whom they are talking instantly know and understand what they're saying. They do not have to work and explain their thoughts to be understood in the ways that we have to. For children, it's not just about learning a new language; it's about figuring out a new way to express themselves. (They have to learn two languages for the one language that we use.) This is why we give names to the first few years of a child's life: the terrible twos, threes, fours, and so on.

This process goes on until children have worked out how to use our slow process of expression and language. It is not a matter of physically growing out of the impatient and rambunctious behavior, but more a matter of when they have learned how to properly use their new set of communication tools. Even as adults, there are times when we hear little voices of frustration and confusion that pop into our heads now and again when we are not understood. But this is a good thing. It reminds us that deep down inside of ourselves—even if we are not aware of it at the present moment—we know that there is an easier way of communicating with one another. This voice or feeling of frustration acts as a gentle reminder of who we really are and where we really came from.

Our physical bodies, because of the delay factor, just need time and repetitive behavior to catch up and remember who we are. When this happens, we can balance both of our bodies—our physical one and our afterlife one—to work in unison. Remember, they are a package. As we explore various activities and create new experiences on earth, the lack of balance in our lives, at times, is because of the continual remembering process we go through. Naturally, it gets easier with time and when both of our bodies fall in sync with each other. Like with anything, the more we practice something, the easier it gets.

After five or six years of learning the basics, we start school. Schools can be like melting pots. Different people all come together for a common goal while expressing themselves as best as they can. It's comparable to mixing various people from all over the world who speak their own languages. Naturally, it's going to be difficult for everyone to communicate properly. This can lead to frustration, miscommunication, etc.

Everyone has difficulty understanding others at one point or another. It's a tiring process and takes up many hours of the day to keep explaining ourselves, desperately trying to be understood in the language we uniquely use. This is why our children sometimes come home from school and say they have had an argument with so-and-so—even if they were best friends a few days before. A typical adult's answer to this would be, "Oh well, it will blow over. You will be friends again tomorrow . . ."

Deep down, adults know in their afterlife bodies that kids argue because they are don't always understand each other. They remember but forget they remember the real reason for this. Why? Because it is still happening with adults, which is why we argue with one another, too. The only way this limited, slow way of communicating would get easier for us would be if we didn't try to get the people around us to talk or understand the ways in which only *we* express ourselves. Instead, we need to learn and adapt to how *they* talk and express themselves. We need to accept everyone in the whole world and realize that we all communicate in our own ways.

It is no wonder why the world, as a whole, is frustrated and living in fear. The media and all the systems encourage us not to remember what we already know deep inside by cloning us and by splitting us up into levels, groups, and sections. Why is this? It's simple. The system doesn't understand the different ways in which we express ourselves. Furthermore, why are people labeled and excluded for expressing themselves using the language they know and the tools and skills that they have? Who is to say that one set of tools is better than another? Why do our systems single out our language abilities, our learning abilities, and our gifts and skills when they do not understand them in the first place?

It is all a veil of illusion that conveniently covers up the many truths and facts that are denied to us as soon as we can walk and talk. We spend a lifetime on earth trying to figure out the system in order to be free to do what we are intended to do in the first place. Only some people are ever lucky enough to wake up and see the bigger picture that surrounds us all. But then they have to jump the many hurdles the system puts in place to try and stop us from being self-expressive. Why do others want to stop us? It's because they are scared of our creations. They can't remember theirs, so they have to control us by weakly attempting to empower themselves so that they don't feel left out in the world.

These folks think that they have to do *something* to fill their time on earth, but they feel like everything inside of themselves is empty and blank. Yet, they see others getting on with their plans. At first, these people get bored doing nothing. But then they get frustrated and angry. They want what creative individuals have. They do everything in their power to make sure that they get bits and pieces of us in one way or another. This is what children do when they take toys from each other. They forget that they both can have the toy by *sharing* it. They get used to taking whatever they want. But while they think that they are being powerful, they actually lose a lot of themselves in the process. When they go back home to the afterlife, they go back the way they came.

The tools they had to explore the earth, including their internal maps, were useless. They never did anything with them; they didn't even try. They were too busy treading on everyone else and taking their creations in any way they desired. They may have been born into their earthly bodies but they go back as the babies they started—as if they never had their own life experiences on earth at all. Remember, no one can take our personal keys away from you. We must try not to let our eyes and ears deceive us into believing that they can.

The truth is our creation will always belong to us. (You will understand exactly what I'm saying when you are back home in the afterlife.) We should not confuse riches with materialism and money; they do not have the same value in the afterlife. Worth is our gold inside of us. It's based on what we create , not by what we take or buy. What is not acknowledged on earth is always acknowledged in the afterlife. Everything is seen and already known. Remember, it's about learning at all levels, not owning.

Furthermore, we shouldn't fear things in life. In the afterlife, there is no shame. There is only understanding and love. Any shame comes from the self. Our experiences guide us and help us to remember the truths. As we slowly begin to remember, we learn more about self-expression in all areas. We also learn more about ourselves.

Wisdom has no beginning or end because it is expanding all the time. It is in everything, including the languages that we use to express our thoughts and feelings. It is not right or wrong or judged. We should think of it as our torches in the dark. Wisdom is everything and nothing at the same time. It is what we want it to be and what we understand and believe. It is not truth. It doesn't consist of laws or rules. Wisdom can be our own footsteps amongst the many footsteps already stepped. Think about it. What does wisdom mean for you?

TEACHINGS

Our earthly experiences split everything up, organizing and putting information into their right file folders and boxes, so to speak. In the afterlife, we do not have to compartmentalize our life experiences. We do not fear that we won't remember something. We don't even have fears that we won't find something if it gets lost. We do not need safes, locks, chains, or anything else security-related. It all goes back to our own personal space. As afterlife people, we do not need security for ourselves. We know we are safe all the time.

But, again, we forget this when we're visiting earth. We believe that what we experience on earth is the truth—that things get lost because that's what we see. We forget our real truth and connection to everything as one. Technically, we can't lose anything in the first place. One reason is because we don't own anything that can be bought with money. Look at all your discarded goods and gifts that perhaps you donated to secondhand shops or charities. Now think about all of the stuff you've tossed out. Weren't most of these items prized possessions that you once owned? If you *owned* them, why did you let go of them? Everything is actually *loaned* to us. These borrowed items aid us with our journeys and experiences on earth.

Another thing that aids us in our personal journeys is our brains. Some of us have the gift of telepathy, or mind reading as it is sometimes called. Most of us are aware that we only use a small percentage of our brains and a fraction of our senses. Half of the time, the ruling elite of the world are making sure we use as little of our true selves as possible so that they can stay in control. Remember, it's a game of empowerment to them.

We are required to get shots when we are born so that our immune systems, which are not developed yet, are weakened. But that's not all. This process is carried on by drugs and cleaning products, pesticides and chemicals. These harmful things are put into everything, including the air. And it's all in the name of money. We are encouraged to buy tobacco, alcohol, and drugs to make our brains addicted to things we shouldn't have. We don't realize what is happening to our immune systems over time. We slowly break down what is supposed to work for us, heal us, and protect us.

In the afterlife, our quick communication abilities are similar to telepathy. But here, mind reading is even more direct and instant. Senses and feelings come into play. We can see things with our afterlife eyes, as well as the full picture—the messages and thoughts. This is something that our physical eyes cannot see. However, it is easy for our afterlife eyes to communicate because we become so in tune with feelings, senses, frequencies, and vibrations. Our body waves of frequency send out particular vibrations of what condition they are in. Sensitive people can tune in to this frequency, too. They are able to pick up the information and then a picture shows itself from the vibrations being received.

Telepathy works not only for communication but for the well-being of the whole body. If we opened up and remembered what we are capable of being, the medical system would go out of business. We would have a lot more healthy people in this world if we decided to take back control of our minds and bodies rather than let the systems have all the control over them. It's sad that we get hooked and even dependent on things that our bodies do not necessarily need to survive. Yet, the systems make us believe that we do need them to function properly.

This is the fear factor. The systems know we are too scared to trust in ourselves. Physically, we would have so much more freedom in every sense of the word if only we would wake up and start remembering the amazing people we really are. We are *so* powerful when we exercise our free will and choice. But, strangely, we give it all away so readily because we have forgotten how powerful we actually are in our own creating. If only we could remember that it's within all of us—and always has been. Alas, the systems know these forgotten secrets. This is why they have so much control over everyone. The illusions of the systems are so convincing because they use fear and money to make us think whatever they want.

The truth is, they can't do this entirely on their own, and that's why they have to have a backup plan with rules, laws, and statute laws all made up by everyday people, like you and me. They want everything to *appear* believable. They are trying to own our power and have control over us. It's not about the things they are physically playing with because, like the rest of us, they may remember some of what we have forgotten but they, too, have forgotten the whole truths of life. Let them play with their toys and argue over them for as long as it takes for them to realize what a waste of time and energy it is.

In the meantime, we should use the magic of *our* free will and choice—the true "real" gold that we all have within. What we trust and believe is for ourselves to decide. It all comes down to our own free will and choice. Do we follow because we believe? Or do we lead because we do not? The decision to follow or lead in our life experiences is entirely up to you . . .

When I learned, or *remembered,* how to talk to the afterlife people, it all began with symbols that were shown to me. It was a bit like what children are taught in elementary school where they are shown pictures of things like an orange for the letter "O," or a picture of a cat with the word, "CAT," under it. Over time, they learn how to put two and two together. Not only do they recognize the picture of a cat, they also equally recognize the associated word. This is how being a messenger began for me. But because I am a visual person, I had lots of different symbols and pictures to work with. Over the years, I eventually figured out how to read and understand the many meanings associated with them. This progressed from pictures to written words, and then later it evolved into thought form. Now I use all of them depending on what the afterlife people are trying to explain and show me. It also depends on what level a particular message is about.

TIME AND SPACE

Simply put, space and time are one line with many vibrations and frequencies in the present. We have categorized and portioned up time into seconds, minutes, hours, days, weeks, months, years, and so on. Within these timeslots, we categorize how we portion our time in the everyday activities that we partake in.

When we are asleep, somewhere around the world others are awake and getting on with their days. All over the world in all different countries we use the same system for what we call and label time. Yet, while we celebrate the New Year at midnight, another country has already celebrated it. We accept that we are never all on the same page when it comes to time. Now I will try to equate the differences in time not from our perspective from our life experiences on earth, but from the afterlife side of the fence.

We are aware of the different timelines we share, even on earth. Time and space are everything and nothing. Depending on the space we're in, and on how we personally interpret time and space, determines our experiences and our perception of time. If a small space is what we believe in and want, that is our creation, and yes, our free will and choice.

Imagine you were born in one room of your house and you grew up and stayed in that one room for all of your earthly life experience. You would not know any different than that room; all of your experiences would have only included that room. Now imagine being born into a family who encourages you to share lots of rooms in the house the next time you have a life experience on earth. You soon realize that your previous conceptions of time and space were much smaller. You had believed through your experience that the one room was all there was. But the second time around, you were able to experience a bigger picture. This is called evolution of time, space, and experience.

This concept grew with our own evolvement until the earth was not enough. Time explored and space entered what we call space and that of the galaxies. Over the years, we have learned how much time and space there is. This is only the surface and the beginning. The more that we allow ourselves to remember, the more we will realize the cycles of life. We will also learn that the life cycles are not time and space like we once thought. In fact, life is creating and evolving all the time. The more we relearn and remember, the more of the magic of life is shown to us through the experiences we ask for. If the simple rules of understanding are not used as a guide while we explore, we then experience the effects of the causes we have created. People will never own the life force of life because they remember so little. They cannot harm it or destroy it because life is eternal.

The effects felt are but a blink of an eye in the great scheme of things, and even these are made up as we go along because we do not understand the basic truths. No one knows any better. We believe these illusions and we live as we are told by the dictators who think they know everything. But we must remember that animals came to the earth to explore before we ever did. We also need to remember that the life force creates and recreates itself for the experiences that we may choose to have.

One day, we will all remember the truths so that we can live in peace and love with everyone else in the afterlife. We will be able to share everything that has been provided for us to enjoy our small space experiences on earth. Remember, we came to the world the same way as everyone else has—naked like a baby. We will go back home the same way except that we will have our experiences to take along with us. The world, time, and space stay where they are.

In the meantime, are you ready to learn about the earthly experiences free will and choice help create while being in the afterlife?

∞

FIFTEEN

Concrete Heaven on Earth

How great is a children's playground? They are full of swings, slides, and climbing frames. It's funny how even these have changed over the years. When I was a kid, our playground was full of wooden equipment to play on—a big contraption of witches' hats, and called a witches' hat. There was a long post in the middle with rows of bars that had seats around it. The seats were all shaped like witches' hats. They spun around the bar and moved up and down. Everything was made of wood. There were even big heavy-duty tires tied to ropes that were used as swings : . .

These days, most playground equipment is made of metal or steel framework. When I lived at the children's home, we used to go over to the fields in the big van that we all traveled in. The giant grassy fields and hills were so much fun. We would spend hours rolling down the hills. There were also lots of berry bushes around. We would go blackberry and gooseberry picking. At the end of the day, we would end up with blackberry stains all over our hands. The staff used to ask who had been eating them, and none of us would ever own up to it. Irritated, they would point to whomever they thought had been eating the berries—which, of course, was all of us—all the while forgetting they could've easily found out by simply looking at our stained fingers and lips.

We use to walk for miles and miles. We'd climb trees. We'd find ladybugs that would crawl up our arms and count the spots on their backs. We'd pick daisies and make daisy chains. We'd pick buttercups and hold them under each other's chins to see who liked butter. We'd wish upon dandelions with their white balls of fluff, blowing the delicate clusters away into the sky.

Summer holidays and half terms would always be spent outside in the fresh, open air. We'd play, run, and hide over and over again until we were so tired we could hardly stand. We often created our own entertainment; it was all we knew. We enjoyed being outdoors. Summertime was our freedom, our outside piece of heaven..

In the wintertime, we stayed inside the house. But we still bundled up in our hand-me-down gear and played outside after we had our tea. It didn't matter what the weather was like. Sometimes an hour on a freezing day felt like a day-and-a-half. Our poor little fingers would be frozen stiff when we got inside. We wouldn't even be able to undo our coats!

After being outdoors for so long, we'd usually have to take baths. Sometimes the staff members would stick two or three of us in one bath. This was sometimes a laugh, depending on who we had to get in the tub with. Some of us made volcanic messes—a turbulent force of nature from the base of the bath. We'd get splashed in our faces over and over again. I would always wait to get out last just so I could see how big the bath actually was. But then the plug would be pulled out from underneath my bum while the on-duty staff member immediately rushed into the other bathroom to do the same with the other tub: one in, one out. They had a little synchronized system going from room to room.

I was scared of the plughole and of the noise it made, sucking the water down as it swirled in circles. I feared that I would be sucked down, too. I would hold on to the sides of the bath—just to make sure I was safe—while I waited to get lifted out of the tub by one of the workers. Relief would wash over me whenever my feet touched the cold bathroom floor.

Bedtime would be the same every night: seven thirty on the dot. It didn't matter if it were spring, summer, autumn, or winter. The cold dark nights were not so bad. But on the hot, long summer days, going to bed when it was still so light outside made nighttime last *forever.* We would often gaze out the window with all of our heads in a row, peeping from under the dark curtains that touched the base of the window frame. We'd watch all the nuns as they walked past into the convent. They reminded me of dominoes.

On weekdays, we'd head straight to school every morning. When we were done with our studies, we'd go back to our rooms and change out of our uniforms for dinner. After we ate, we'd all be responsible for clearing the plates and tables, leaving the dining area sparkling clean.

One night, I had a Girl Scout meeting; I was in the Brownies group. With my brown uniform on and big bows in my hair, and my brown glasses falling halfway down my nose, I skipped eagerly to the front door. The meeting was to be held across the street from the children's home.

But, like always, a bunch of us wanted to be first to the meeting. We all ran as fast as we could toward the hall. I ran so fast that my feet slipped, slid, and tripped across the gravel. In a matter of seconds, I fell hard, landing heavy on both of my knees. The stinging sensation felt like I had just been stung by a million bees.

Embarrassed, I slowly stood up, wincing at the severe pain. Both knees oozed blood. It dripped down my legs, staining my socks. My knees were all black and full of dirt and more blood.

Not knowing what to do, I ran back to the staff. They sat me down on the countertop in the kitchen and mopped up all of the blood for me. It took a while, but at least I didn't need a cast or anything. However, I did need a few bandages. When I was all patched up, I hobbled back to the Brownies meeting. Of course, my favorite game was being played. The girls had created two long rows of "ladders" with their legs outstretched, touching feet to feet. Each team had to take turns running down the leg ladder. Whatever team finished first would win. The Brownies leader took one look at my bandaged knees and suggested that I sit on a chair and watch everyone else. Watching Brownies play and interact with one another was *not* the same as taking part in the activities. Still, at least I didn't miss the meeting!

Those were the days of playgrounds past—of carefree summers, outdoors adventures, wooden playgrounds, and scraped knees. But soon I was entering another kind of playground: my teenage years. They appeared before I knew it. The playground I began frequenting was the swimming pool with my close friends. That became our new playground fun. The chlorine stung our eyes, making them red and sore, but it was worth it to splash about. We lounged on pool floats and gossiped, enjoying the sun's warm rays. Later, we'd have a long walk back home with soaking wet hair. Again, we didn't mind. We were happy to be outside and free.

We'd walk past the many brick buildings that stood all in line. We'd pass the numerous roads and side streets that all looked the same—paved, bricked, or pebble-dashed. The flowers blew in the gentle breeze among the blades of grass on the front lawns. Everyone silently competed with each other to have the best-manicured yards, the prettiest flowers, and the greenest grass. Their lawns were always cut neat with no weeds to be seen. We felt safe walking through these neighborhoods.

Flash forward to having children of my own. I walk up the hill to the library and past the many rows of houses that are now all changed. They are still all bricked and painted, but they are protected with big metal gates. Once quaint little neighborhoods now look like mini parking lots. Tiny tufts of weeds show where grass and flowers used to be. Houses and gardens have all turned to stone. The fields where we used to play are all gone; big brick apartment buildings now stand in their places. Of course, there is a big parking garage there, too, to hold the metal cars that are now plenty used.

The green grass and fresh air are now all covered in concrete, brick, or stone. It's no wonder why kids can't breathe very well these days. All the fumes from cars whizzing by have something to do with it. In fact, the ozone layer is depleting at an alarming rate because we have very little grass and trees to help sustain it.

The earth once made up of pastures of the land—with the tides of the sea, the lakes, and rivers flowing by—made a playground for children to explore. Those days have disappeared before our very eyes. It was a gradual change as each year quietly passed us by. But it's so obvious if we remember back to our childhood days that are now only memories, if not altogether forgotten.

The earth is different than it used to be. Sometimes, we forget that we are responsible for changing it. Our planet is covered in bricks, concrete, stone, paved floors, tarmac roads, and trash. All that's left are a few trees, a few fields, and a few rivers and streams. The once plentiful land has turned. The scales of life are out of balance, yet we wonder why we have more viruses and breathing problems than we used to. The answers stare us in the face. Look around at the world in which we live—at the concrete, the metal signs, the railings, and barriers that wrap around the roads. Examine the surface of the earth; the towns and cities weigh it down and puts pressure on it. The vast open space the earth used to be has shrunk into a mass of suffocating heavy construction.

All of the concrete and unnecessary pollution are slowly smothering and suffocating us. Animals and insects are losing the homes they used for centuries at rapid speeds. We don't think about that. We only think about and see dollar signs. We forget that the surface of the earth needs to breathe, just like us. Our oxygen isn't as good as it used to be. Now a lot of us need to rely on inhalers. These devices used to never exist. Why do we need them now? Why do we keep damaging our planet? Ask the builders and businesspeople who have literally taken the green of the land and covered it up with concrete. They are responsible for making us sick. They are putting toxins in our air so that we can't breathe. What effects do you think earth's surface feels? Like the cogs of a wheel coming undone, it was only a matter of time before the earth buckled under the strain of the destruction we've been causing for so long. This is not how life began; this was not life's long-made plans. We have not learned to mix and live with grass because, sadly, we have not seen its true worth.

It's only a matter of time before the earth's surface cracks. This will cause stored gases to be released after years and years of build up of pressure underneath. Why, then, do we wonder why the weather has just recently begun to change so drastically? Why do we wonder why the earth has volcanoes? Why do we wonder why the earth's sea rises so high? Why do we wonder why mudslides occur? Why do we wonder why nature reacts at all? It's because the earth can't breathe! This is our planet's way of talking back, to let us know that it is on the move. The earth wants to change back to what it knows: a land of grass, trees, and flowers. It wants to be home to insects and wildlife (which came before humankind) again. We have to learn to live with what's known—with what the earth knows and is comfortable with—instead of making money. If we don't, we're going to find ourselves in a heap of trouble.

We need to take a good long look at our paved gardens, our metal fronted house gates, and the blocks upon blocks of apartments and business buildings. The metal, stone, and concrete structures and fittings we have made have put tremendous unwanted pressure on the earth. We need to stop looking up at the smoggy skies and wondering why the world is reacting the way it is. Instead, we need to look outside and remember the land we once knew and loved. The earth will find a way to breathe again; it's bigger than any of us ever will be. But if we don't change the way we think and act soon, we won't be able to complain when the earth starts knocking down our buildings in the form of natural disasters because it will be our own fault. We've been ignoring or turning a blind eye to what is truly precious for far too long now.

We need to open our eyes and stop fighting over the land that is left, only to take it and put up a concrete wall or metal gate to keep our materialistic possessions safe. What good will money be if the earth starts to crumble? We've had our fun; we will soon listen to nature if we don't change our ways now. The earth will survive with the animals and the trees. It's humankind that will fall like dominoes because of all of the concrete that currently covers the land.

This is how I see our land—our concrete heaven on earth. Is this how you imagine heaven to be? I will leave it up to you to decide . . .

∞

SIXTEEN

Guided Afterlife Tour—Healing Medicine, Gardens, Animals, and Plants

As we mature, our ways of doing things and being things start to change, and so do our attitudes. We let go of things that once were so important to us. I am sure you have heard the saying used by many adults, "I have mellowed over the years." Why do we feel this way as we get older? Is it because our bodies get worn down and we think we can't keep going at the same pace we once functioned at? As we slow down, we begin to have more opportunities and more time to spend with and on ourselves. This is why we find ourselves laughing and saying things like, "Oh! I sound just like my mom!" We start doing the things our parents did when they got older.

I know I have changed my outlook more in the last two to three years of my life. My whole routine has changed. Different things mean more to me than they did before. Now, my life is not just about survival or sorting so much out. Yes, I will always have jigsaw pieces to sort out from time to time; that never stops I guess. After all, life presents us with new things to explore all the time, especially within ourselves. These days, I am more interested in the well-being connection between my two bodies and the connections between nature and animals. Although the animals we share our homes with are regarded as great pets and companions, I know that there is so still much more to learn about them.

This reminds me of a story. We had two kittens that we bought a few weeks apart from the same shop. Their personalities were completely different from each other. I noticed one was a young soul and the other one was quite a bit wiser. One day, the kitten with the young soul had just enjoyed her dinner and then went outside. About half an hour later, there was a knock on the door. The poor kitten had just been run over and died. Of course, we were upset and buried her in the garden.

We wanted another playmate for our one remaining kitten, but I was skeptical about getting another kitten because of the busy road. So instead, we got a six-month-old puppy. We brought her home and my kitten and the new puppy played together in such a way that it was crazy to think that one animal was a dog and the other was a cat! They mixed and played as equals.

One night, we were in bed when our cat came and snuggled up on my pillow above my head. She lay with her body all curled up around my head all night. It got my attention because in all the years we had known her, this was something she never did. The next morning, we began getting ready for the day. I dropped my kids off at school and no sooner had I returned that the cat began rubbing herself all around my legs and getting under my feet. Clearly, she was trying to get my attention.

Being in a rush to get dinner cooked, I put her food down for her on the floor, thinking that was what she wanted. She looked at it and still kept fussing around me. Again, this was out of character for her. As I continued to cook, she suddenly jumped up on the edge of the countertop nearest to the stove. There, she just stared at me for about ten minutes. This strange behavior was also something she never did. *Does she want to go outside?* I wondered to myself, completely confused. So, I let her out . . .

About half an hour later, there was a knock on the door. Our beloved cat had been run over and had died. We were devastated. *Two* cats? Yet, in hindsight, I wonder if her strange behavior was her way of trying to get my attention to say goodbye. It was like she knew it was her time to go back home. I wish I had not been so busy that evening. Still, I know by her actions and extreme displays of affection that she appreciated us as much as we appreciated her.

That left us with our dog who proved to be equally amazing. And while I really didn't want to have any more pets after the drama with the cats, I knew that other plans were in store for our family. Soon, my eldest daughter got a puppy—the same breed as ours. But due to her circumstances, she was unable to keep her. So, yes, you guessed it! I took her in and, thankfully, my other dog took her under her wing, looking after her like the mommy she now has become. They play, mirror, and follow each other everywhere. In fact, our newest addition to our family does what our other cat used to do! This is an example of how things live on. Lately, we have been focusing our energy on trying to learn about growing fruits and vegetables. I feel that nature and all it provides is our medicine of life.

Before we changed our way of eating and cooking, my husband used to suffer from acid reflux because of a hernia he had. He used to take tablets for this and tablets for that. But this past year, our family was able to wean itself off of our dependency on tablet forms of healing. We started off gradually by changing what we eat and how we cook. We tried to use ingredients that were natural. Now my husband doesn't need all the tablets he once took. In fact, he doesn't even suffer from his old ailments anymore. It was what he was putting inside his body that caused him all the trouble. We now use Olbas Oil for our headaches and sore muscles. Although, my youngest, who is only twelve years old, cannot use this as a rub; instead, she uses Head Soothe Wellness Oil.

I am not educated on herbs or alternative methods, but I am now willing to invest time and energy into learning more about them based on the results I have seen. We should allow our bodies to work as they are intended to work. We should encourage our immune systems to stay strong and work harder for us when we are ill. A lot of us have been reliant on tablets for much too long. I am not saying stop taking tablets altogether. I'm just saying we should look into embracing a healthy, active lifestyle and utilize the tools of our body. We should nourish our bodies with offerings from nature instead of opting for pills or other quick fix potions. I mean, we are so programmed to put junk into our bodies. We don't really stop and think about the problems these things can cause us—immediately and down the road. I think the best way to live is to work on ourselves from the inside out. Only then can we truly move forward.

We all have heard about healing medicine, hands on healing, chakras, and meditation. These are all tools in which to find a connection with our true source and energy vibrations that connect everything. Personally, I believe that healing is within and without, flowing through everything that is. Why do I think this is so? Because healing comes from the same place the connection of talking to dead people comes from, but in an expanded vibration that emanates around it. For example, think about how the air we breathe in is around us *and* within us. That is what healing is like. It is in everything. It isn't just contained in one spot or a few spots in the body. These tools are used to silence the mind so we can focus on something that is not physical. Healing is in every space of every living thing and in every cell that ever is.

After all, we hear of absent healing. So how does the healing coming up out of the chakras and go find someone else halfway across the world when we have to use planes, trains, and other forms of transportation to get there? The answer is about connection and tuning in to the frequency of the person and that of the healing vibration. It's kind of like what happens with our telephone wires. We are able to send our thoughts and messages via these lines to anyone in the world as long as they have a connection. This is how healing is given and equally received—free. It is not contained in a box or in a specific place. These things are just to aid the physical connection.

Everything has been provided for us to live a life of well-being and experience on earth. All the plants and nature are around us for a reason. Unfortunately, however, the government can't make a profit on these natural resources. So, over the years, we have been conditioned to rely on tablets that the government makes and provides. It uses only a small fraction of the true healing ingredients; the rest is just filler and additives. As time goes on, the government takes more and more of the healing ingredients out, making them so diluted that we end up with tablets that have so many chemicals and ingredients in them that we then end up with other illnesses!

Healing comes from what we trust and believe in and what works for us. We rely on our own free will and choice. How much credit do we give our bodies for working properly? How much do we allow our bodies to work against us out of fear? Again, ultimately this is for us to decide for ourselves. As a general example, I often felt that celebrity Jade Goody was enjoying her life and her experiences. But as soon as a label such as cancer was given to her, she changed. She then began entrusting her life to the hands of the professionals. As soon as she began having her treatments, her body got weaker and weaker. I believe this happened because of the treatments, not because of the cancer.

Her immune system had been so badly weakened after the treatments. And quite often, it is not the cancer that kills the person, but the effects the treatment has upon the body.

Again, fear dictates. I do wonder if the physical body was not invaded by such treatments that people would have a better quality of life than that which is offered—to see how the body heals itself. We do hear of miracles and it leaves the doctors baffled with no answers as to why. If only we would give our bodies a chance to heal within the many layers that we are.

We have the opportunity to experience so much more than the physical body is capable of experiencing on its own. If only we would allow and trust our bodies to work for us the way they are supposed to. Nature came first on earth for a reason. It is only our meddling in something that we have forgotten and don't understand that has caused us to be in so much pain and reliant on so many drugs. Sadly, we tend to only understand money and power.

We need to remember our gifts and skills and all that we're about. We are who we are for a reason. It is our responsibility to find and work out our own reasons and meanings that go on to aid our choices and the experiences that we have. We've all heard the sayings, "You are what you eat" and "Be careful what you wish for." We hold the keys to our own creations, wishes, and desires pertaining to the things we wish to experience. This rings true no matter what side of the fence we are on. They all lead to the same front door. The only difference is our own personal free will and choice on which rooms we want to explore and visit and how much we want to understand. It's a big home that we all live in, isn't it? Yes, home is where the heart is . . . in life and in love.

∞

SEVENTEEN

Guided Afterlife Tour—Socializing/Activities (Layers versus Pairs Equals Experience)

When I was in school, children were seen as students with different abilities and accepted the way they were. Society has changed since then. The education system seems to be more all about being a business rather than a learning institute to actually educate, help, and nurture children with skills not only on an educational level, but on an emotional level, too. I have seen teachers and witnessed how communication between teachers and pupils has deteriorated over the past twenty-something years since I have had children of my own. It saddens me that schools miss the point on how important this is. People skills should always come first, followed by the teaching.

For example, I went to college to learn about Indian head massage when I was in my late thirties. My class had a great teacher who not only taught us the subject but made sure we really knew the subject deeper than just the basic facts. Then I went on to study reflexology. This teacher was only interested in whether or not we passed the exam; she wanted her records of achievements to be good. For her, it was about quantity, not *quality*. We all passed, yet I left not knowing anything about reflexology. To this day, I still don't really know much about it. I have a piece of paper to show I have passed the course, and I can even go on to get a job in the field. Out of common sense, I will not attempt to do so. I know I don't know anything more than the front cover of the textbook we used. I took the exams and passed the course but the quality and actual knowledge was missing.

Luckily, I can incorporate the *very* basic concepts I learned in the reflexology course with the quality I got out of the Indian head class and combine them with Reiki and healing. However, all of this only touches the surface. In literal terms, it only deals with the bones, muscles, and systems of the physical body. Well, what about working with the afterlife body? How do our traditional teachings touch the afterlife body when they only work with the surface of the physical one?

My guide, Ramini, knows the traditional way in which we do things here on earth when it comes to healing and massage. Knowing my frustration about this, Ramini taught me how to work with the afterlife body as well. This is called "pulse magnetic massage." It touches the surface of the physical body and that of the afterlife body; both bodies are then able to be worked on. And yes, I do feel this has been known for centuries because it is something we feel, sense, and tune in to. I was happy I could now work on the whole body versus just one part of it. I love the fact that the method I use works inside out and not outside in. The only aftercare you need is your breathing.

Actual *experience* is worth so much more than degrees, labels, or certificates. Sure, these pieces of paper may look good and sound impressive but if we don't have experience, these pieces of paper are not worth much more than just that: paper. On the flip side, without a piece of paper to validate what we know, all the experience in the world will not be recognized within the systems that are put in place.

Think back to when you were in school. Do you remember how all the children would pair off or start socializing in different groups, or cliques? I know I found this confusing. I didn't understand why everyone just didn't all get along. At the time, I had a best friend who I had been close with for years. We shared all our thoughts and feelings with each other. But one day, my friend suddenly ditched me and started hanging out with another friend. What had I done? Why didn't she want me as her best friend anymore?

My comfortable and familiar routine had suddenly changed overnight. It hurt each time I saw my friend laughing with her new best friend. However, I soon realized why this had happened: Her new best friend was very popular. She also always brought candy to school. On top of that, she'd often give out little gifts, like nice pens, to students. I could not match this because of my personal situation. There was nothing I could do except accept the hard fact that people change.

A year later, however, my best friend wanted me back as her best friend. Apparently, her previous candy-bribing best friend could not support her emotional needs. On top of that, her former best friend became pregnant at fourteen; she soon left the school to have her baby. My old best friend didn't have anything anymore—not her so-called upgrade of a best friend or the gifts she used to receive. Part of me wanted to give our friendship another try—I had liked her so much before—but the other part of me felt like I was now second best. I doubted how much I could trust our friendship. Besides, I had already moved on and made another new best friend who enjoyed me for me, not for what I could buy her.

We can see how groups and friends can change and affect our lives and the situations and experiences in which we find ourselves, depending on how the situation touches us emotionally. This governs the way in which we react to it, and that of our attitudes toward it. We have all have heard the saying, "Two's company and three's a crowd!" This is because we become so busy trying to learn the new language of the second person that a third person is almost impossible to handle. In short, multiple people interacting becomes too much for us to understand and work out.

All of that potential drama only involves friends. Think about how we deal with and communicate with our family members! If we do not spend the time to understand our unique language on earth, we will ultimately end up fighting a lot. This shows how much we do not comprehend. Oftentimes, we do not express ourselves the way we want to. If we find ourselves struggling to communicate at home with our families, it is no wonder it is hard to understand the many other people we mix with and meet as we go on with our day-to-day activities.

Speaking of outsiders, gangs are an entirely different group. They can have different intentions, depending on why the members are in a gang in the first place. We usually associate gangs as not being very nice. We tend to think of violence, crime, and fear. Running into a gang can be equivalent to experiencing a car crash—but with people. We never know what to expect or how hurt we could get. On the other hand, there are gangs consisting of members who are trying to better themselves. They thrive on creativity and use their initiative and imaginations in a positive way. These members are attempting to offer value to their gangs and to society, in general, because they want to experience value inside of themselves.

We often feel safer and included when we are part of a group, be it a group of friends, a close-knit family, or even a gang. No one ever wants to feel isolated or alone. From a young age, and especially during our school years, we are encouraged to join groups—social groups, sports groups, music groups, etc. I remember receiving school reports and it was regarded as "bad" if students didn't belong to some kind of a club. With so much going on in my dysfunctional home life and personal space, I didn't have the time, energy, or interest in adding one more thing to my already heavy load. I just put anything on the form to fit in—anything to be accepted. Even a little bit of acceptance would have been helpful at the time. Simply saying that I was involved and included made my teachers leave me alone. It gave me a bit of space to attempt to start sorting things out in my life; my experiences were piling up into an unmanageable mess.

At times, I felt like I was dragging around a heavy suitcase wherever I went. This caused me to worry. Everything was just *so* confusing. My life felt like a thousand-piece jigsaw puzzle. I knew at some point I would have to stop everything and spend some time (or, in my case, years) attempting to sort all the pieces out. It got to the point where I had to take action. As I slowly put the pieces in the right order—carefully prioritizing the things in my life that I wanted to hold on to and discarding the baggage I didn't want to carry anymore—I then started to see the whole picture begin to emerge. I sorted each piece out and the feelings that matched the many experiences. Finally, I began to understand my life and all of its experiences. And you know what? It didn't look that bad.

I suddenly realized how all of my experiences—positive and negative—played a part in my life story. When pieced together, it all made sense. It is when we split these pieces up and deny ourselves these pieces that the pattern replays itself through different situations. Yet, with the same meaning through them and no matter what piece is replayed through a different experience, it *still* does not make sense until it is pieced together as a whole—until the jigsaw puzzle is complete. Only then, after a little effort, can we see the picture that has always been there.

LAYERS VS. PAIRS = EXPERIENCE

Growing up, I used to enjoy playing a game of cards called "Pairs." Generally speaking, when we play cards, the first thing we usually do is shuffle them to mix them up. Then we deal them out and play our games. However, in Pairs, we have to lay all the cards out on the table, facedown. We take turns flipping over one card and then another one to see if we have a pair. Usually, the players who do not get very many matches get bored and want to give up. Deep down, it is not the game that has made them feel this way, it is the feelings that they have inside.

Cards are similar to our life experiences. Many cards can be compared to many layers of our situations and circumstances that match various feelings, depending on the experiences we choose to have. When we are trying to find ourselves within the many hands of cards we are dealt, we should remember to lay the cards of our lives on a table in front of us and see what kind of matches we come up with. Matches will give us the meaning we are looking for.

I use this technique in my readings. As with playing cards or putting together a jigsaw puzzle, the first thing we do is to tip all the pieces out and start sorting them out into order. This example mirrors the pieces of us. They are all connected. If we are trying to sort out an experience that has affected us in any way—be it physically, mentally, emotionally, or direction and function—we need to remember the layers of pairs that are connected to the experience. Everything combined is called a *package*.

Emotions and feelings are what experiences are in truth. It is not the doing or the act, but the *beingness* of the depth of feeling that has impacted us and our feelings. For some of us, going about our days is strictly about doing, or getting a job done. This is acting out activities on autopilot. This happens when the connection of our feelings is denied for whatever reason.

We are familiar with the saying, "Big boys don't cry." This teaches boys who grow into men not to feel or express how they feel. But actions and experiences are always connected as a package with feelings. Feelings cannot be shut off, so to speak. They have to come out some way, otherwise it's like we're holding our breath forever. But when we don't have the ability to actively express our feelings, we may choose to deal with them in another way—by hiding them with another action.

Some people become workaholics. Some may become gamblers. Others may find an addiction to focus on, like plastic surgery or, worse, drugs. Some folks may isolate themselves from others on purpose. We can keep running away and hiding or making excuses for the way we feel, but this is hard work. We will ultimately burn ourselves out. It's so much easier to face the truth of who we really are. And even if we don't burn ourselves out, situations and circumstances will eventually catch up with us; they always do. Soon, the suppression of our feelings weighs on us so much that it begins to affect our *doingness*. It is strange how one saying, or belief, has the ability to change our attitudes and confine us to a life of hiding and being on the run—from ourselves.

These are just examples and metaphors on how we play our cards of our lives. We either choose to play our hands guarded and close to our chests or spread out on the table exposed for all to see.

Technically, the latter way of living is how we began our lives as newborns. We all cried and screamed. We dribbled and soiled ourselves. But none of that mattered. We passed no judgment toward ourselves or others. We accepted people for who they were and loved them back unconditionally. In fact, we didn't know any different. When do we change and start judging ourselves and others? When we do not look at people and accept them for who they are? It seems like this all changes as soon as we learn to speak a language and then spend a lifetime trying to understand it.

No wonder life is so confusing and made so complicated by us all! There are so many layers to have to piece together in order for anything to make sense. There are so many opinions, outcomes, and choices. I am not surprised that we often feel like we are pulled in various directions, from pillar to post. We become attached to our cards of life, so to speak, because we spend so much time and effort trying to figure them out. We put so much energy into them that we become emotionally invested and do not want to let go, even if it is in our best interest to do so. The main problem becomes us not being able to find a matching pair. We are unable to let go of something emotionally because we only let go of the situation.

Being able to sort out our own personal packs of cards involves being self-aware and recognizing what cards of experiences actually belong to *us* and what cards belong to *someone else*. With each situation come layers of actions; with these actions come the layers of feelings associated with that particular experience and action. It is not about just sorting out the action that created the situation; it's also about where the situation came from, who it belongs to, and the feelings that come with it.

All of these components are connected as one package, as I mentioned earlier. Sometimes, we will say, "Oh, I sorted out that problem years ago!" or "Oh, I let that go already. It's time for me to move on." But do we sort out and let go of *all* the layers connected with these experiences, or just the main event? This is why, in life, past problems keep coming up to the surface in our different situations and experiences that we have. We haven't fully let go yet. We need to look for the common thread running through all the different situations that make these occurrences keep coming up. They are gentle wake-up calls that something we experienced in the past has not been sorted out within its layers.

By remembering that we have many layers, we can understand how to sort them out properly and *really* let go. When we let go completely, we allow ourselves to move on to our next experiences without dragging unfinished business along with us. Our proverbial baggage stays light. Naturally, all of this can take time and effort to do the right way. Sometimes, we need to stop what we are doing and change our familiar routines and patterns.

If we don't stop and try to compose ourselves, we may get so burnt out and worn out that we end up physically ill under the strain. Having a stressed out lifestyle can wreak havoc on our bodies, physically and mentally. Stopping allows us to sort out our problems, recollect our thoughts, and, most importantly, heal. Even if it means spending a little more time by ourselves or taking a small vacation to get away from the busy flow of life, we should do it. We should make time to feel balanced.

Yes, separating ourselves from the rest of the world can feel isolating and lonely. We are so used to being squashed together amongst everyone else, or being plugged in to our iPods, computers, and cell phones. To be in our *own* personal space can, at first, feel like meeting a stranger for the first time, or a long-lost friend we've lost touch with. But we have to remember that this so-called stranger in us has been with us since we began our live experiences on earth. In fact, it will be with us for all eternity. We never lost the *real* us; we just tend to forget where we are.

And while we're on the topic of isolation, being singled out for a special skill or gift the media can benefit from can make us feel good. On the other hand, being singled out because we are not of the same class or group as someone else who thinks he or she is superior can make us feel badly about ourselves. As I was growing up in the children's home, I definitely felt different—an outcast. The truth is that others did not understand where I came from, and with misunderstanding comes fear. Everyone else had "normal" homes with mothers and fathers. I had none of this and was shunned for it.

When we are isolated for any given period of time, we can begin to feel invisible. We start thinking, *If I am not seen or heard, then maybe the problem will go away on its own. I do not understand these people and they do not understand me. Therefore, I do not want to deal with them or what comes with associating with them. I am too busy sorting myself out.* This is an example of how we find ourselves in one situation that then rolls us into another situation, depending on the reactions we receive from others pertaining to ourselves. If we are different from others, we run the risk of being misunderstood and judged. If we are too skilled or gifted, or if we stand out physically or mentally, we are judged because we are not normal or familiar. But what actually is considered "normal" when we are so multi-layered, anyway?

I will give you an example of contradicting prejudice. Along my journey of experiences, I became friends with a person labeled a "black man." To me, he was simply a person, but hey, everyone and everything has to have labels, right? Well, this friend of mine had a mother who was labeled "white" and a dad who was labeled "black." My friend, confused by the prejudices that he faced because he was not pure white or black, often felt angry and hurt by what prejudices had created through history. These prejudices, passed down from generation to generation, made him question who he really was. On meeting his nephew and niece (who had the same parents), I noticed how different they were; the nephew was pure white—whiter than me. However, their dad was black and the niece was a different shade of black. My point is that our physical eyes may not always see the true reflection of what actually is.

To all the people who are upset because of another person's skin color, and to those who fight and go to war over something as trivial as this, remember that a white person's skin color may actually be black; it's just that your eyes cannot see it. This is how our eyes and ears can deceive us. We assume too much and pass judgment on others based on what we physically see and hear. Sadly, mere illusions tend to govern how we are treated and treat others. Remember, when we all started as babies, none of this mattered. We played and accepted each other for who we are, not by what we look like.

We spend so much time, energy, and money on how we look, but for what? When we move on to the afterlife side of the fence, we no longer need our physical vehicles anymore. Look inside an urn after a cremation at all of the ashes or inside a grave at all the bones and tell me what each person looked like. What was their skin color? How much does that matter? Remember, we all go back home the way we came here—the same. Our only differences—the real stuff that matters—is what's inside and what we can't see: our experiences and our essence.

Ever since I have been able to "see dead people," as it is labeled, I have been called a witch and a freak. I am called these names simply because I am different. It doesn't matter that I still experience everything in this lifetime like everyone else. Either way, being different allows me to share so many of my unique stories with those who want to listen.

We join various groups, classes, religions, etc., because we're told to do so from a young age. It's the norm, according to what we read or are shown through the media. If we don't join groups—if we go against the grain, so to speak—we run the risk of being labeled as loners, strange, weird, or odd. Again, these labels are only used when we do not understand someone.

All the greatest inventions and works of art in the world are usually made and created by these types of people—the so-called freaks. Sadly, we do not realize how extraordinarily talented they are until after they have passed. .How many people have become famous and appreciated and understood more only *after* they have passed? The world and the people in it had to catch up to these "freaks"; they were all ahead of their time. Despite the ridicule and criticism these magnificent inventors and artists may have received, they left behind amazing gifts for us to (eventually) understand. We should be grateful and learn from our mistakes.

It is ironic that after their deaths, their labels changed to "genius." Tools, contraptions, and works of art that used to be scrutinized and made fun of are now prized possessions worth millions of dollars that are hanging in museums and art galleries around the world. Everything is valuable no matter which way we look at it. There is always something to learn in the journey of life on earth.

Sometimes, isolation is a personal choice out of free will. These people remember the map of intentions that they came to the earth with. They remember they have their maps and want to use them. They shut themselves away to find their creations—their purpose—within themselves. They are not distracted by the confusion outside of themselves because they remember their keys and choose to use them. While some may call these people loners or freaks, I call them wise. They knew what they wanted out of life and didn't have to go searching to find their happiness.

There will always be many ways of looking at things in everything we see and experience. These ways can positively or negatively affect our attitudes. What do you own that is your own choice of reflection? Who are you and what are you all about? Does your reflection mirror everyone else's attitudes toward life or your own? Being true to ourselves is the best gift we can reward ourselves with. Without being ourselves, we get lost and mixed up by acting like others who we are not. Life is to be enjoyed, but we can only enjoy it if we allow ourselves to break free from the chains and use our internal keys to do so.

∞

EIGHTEEN

UNEXPLAINED LIFE

I have called this chapter "Unexplained Life" rather than "Unexplained Phenomena" because, to me, the afterlife of our life—whether remembered or not—is about life, regardless of if we understand it or not. When we are ready to understand, when we have reached an understanding of *why* we experience life, then we eventually get the answers to it. Life is ours inside, not outside ourselves. The outside of ourselves is our view and understanding because of how our physical eyes see the physical world of earthly experiences.

This reminds me of a recurring dream I had as a child. It is as vivid today as when I first experienced it. I had this dream many times from the age of seven. Looking back, I understand the dream more now, especially now that I know how to pick up on subtle cues because of working as a medium. I remember walking down the local street outside the children's home. This particular road was a busy main road that led to some shops—one being our local candy shop. What a shop it was! There were glass jars and shelves full of bags of Golden Nugget chewing gum in drawstring bags, Gobstoppers. Sherbet, and many halfpence sweets, to name a few.

As I walked down that familiar road, I passed many people. And while I went by each person, I felt naked, as if I stood out like an alien. The strange thing was that I had a hole right through my middle. People could see right through me! I felt so self-conscious of the gaping hole in my stomach in my dream and could not understand why I was the only one who looked this way. I tried to hide the hole with my hands and arms. Even stranger, no one said anything or noticed. They were too busy getting on with their own lives.

I had this unusual dream on and off for many years. Each time, I would experience the same details and the same feelings. It was as if the same film was being shown to me over and over again. The dream, itself, didn't frighten me; it just made me feel naked . . . and odd. I didn't like the fact that I seemed to be made differently than everyone else. I didn't want to look different. After all, it's clearly not normal for a physical body to have a hole straight through the middle of it. Still, I accepted the bizarre dream for what it was and shrugged, knowing how crazy dreams can be. Over the years, I have managed to realize the difference between dreams and dream state visions, or messages. Now I know even dreams can feel real, but I noticed there is one big difference between a dream and a vision.

When I dream that I am *me* and I'm mixing with whomever or whatever is in the dream, that is a regular dream—parallel, so to speak, like being here face-to-face with someone. However, when a dream vision occurs, it is like two of me are present. Not only am I experiencing the dream face-to-face with whomever or whatever is in the dream, there is also another side to me who observes it and watches it at the same time. Basically, I can watch myself in a dream and also experience it. During the experience, it all feels quite normal and so I accept it.

It's only when we experience earth twofold do we notice the difference. For example, imagine you are a flat piece of paper, folded in two. This is how we tend to experience earth. Yet, we all know a piece of paper can be folded more times than twice. Still, we choose to live our lives in a twofold way: cause and effect. But what happens if we open our minds to more than a twofold life and open up our sixth sense ability past the door of talking to the dead? What if we branch off into the sixth sense of the self (our afterlife bodies)? Folding the piece of paper a third time enables another side of ourselves to see, sense, and ultimately speak to the dead. If we fold the same paper a fourth time, we are able to explore more of the atmosphere of life, such as travel into other dimensions. In a way, the piece of paper never stops folding during our many life experiences. The constant folding represents an evolvement of life inside of us.

Let's go back a bit. Imagine that our piece of paper has progressed into three folds. What happens when we unfold the piece of paper? Well, if we have folded it three times, there should be three folds, right? No. Once we open the three times folded piece of paper, we can count eight squares within the folds. If we fold the paper only once—because we see life on earth from the *two* sides of the fence—and then open it up and lay it flat, the paper as a whole sheet still shows two sides, not just one.

In a way, we are similar to pieces of paper. This analogy shows what we *think* we are on the surface. But opened up, we clearly have many parts, sides, and facets. It's not until we take a peek inside and unravel and open ourselves up do we then see and experience more than we thought we originally could. The more we unravel—either through our dreams or communicating with the afterlife people—the more we understand and experience so much more than what our physical lives have to offer.

I once took an art class in school where the students were all given a piece of paper. The teacher held up her piece of paper to the class, but it looked nothing like ours. Hers had many cutout people holding hands in a long line, like a link chain. Puzzled, we all waited for her instructions. She smiled and said, "Today, class, I want you to make one of these!" Holding my flat piece of paper, I had no idea how to shape it to look like hers. However, after a few minutes of trying to figure it out, our teacher showed us each step. She taught us how to fold the paper many times and draw a half figure on the front by cutting a certain way. When we were done cutting out our people shapes, we carefully opened up our creations to see the same chain link of people our teacher had originally presented to us! It felt like magic, creating something so intricate out of a simple piece of paper.

Even if we view and see life as flat—like a single sheet of paper—I would like you to look at your blank piece of paper and imagine the earth on it. Think about where you have lived and the various paths you have personally traveled down to get to where you are today. Remember, there are at least two sides to every story. Turn the piece of paper over; that is the other half of you. Think of the second side as your afterlife body. It will always be there.

Maybe there is more to life than that of what we experience on earth. Think about all of the times you've had unexplained feelings . . . or when the hairs on the back of your neck or arms randomly stand up on end. Think about when the phone suddenly rings and the person on the other line is a friend whom you were just thinking about. The silent page of the other side of us surfaces every now and then. It is during these sporadic times that we remember both sides that we are, when we remember that we have two bodies, not one. These moments undoubtedly awaken our curiosity.

This takes me to a personal experience of life's unexplained happenings. Many years ago, I gave my bedroom to my daughter. My partner and I slept on the floor in the living room, which meant I had to make up two of those foldout foam beds on the floor. I put the bottom sheet down to cover both beds to create a double bed. Then, placing the pillows on top, I laid out the quilt. We turned the lights out and attempted to go to sleep. My partner and I both slipped under the quilt; the cotton bottom sheet felt nice and snug. But the next morning, I woke up rather startled. Both of my arms were placed neatly down by each side of my body, and I could hardly move. Somehow, the covers had been tucked tight from my neck down to my feet. I felt like an Egyptian mummy!

And it got stranger. I noticed that I was also now *under* the bottom sheet. My body was touching the rough foam bed instead! *How can this be?* I thought, completely confused. I gently woke up my partner to look at me. He was still on top of the bottom sheet. That made me even more baffled. *How could I have ended up like this and not wake him up? .I do not sleep walk! Yet, here I am, tucked in head to toe!* I thought. To this day, I still don't know what happened that night.

Many unexplained experiences have occurred in my life. I remember a few years back, when I used to smoke, that I was driving in my car by myself. I had lit a cigarette while in the car and began smoking it. When it was almost gone, I went to throw the butt out the window, only to find it had been blown back inside the vehicle by the wind! I had new trousers on and was alarmed to realize I was now sitting on my cigarette butt. I immediately began to panic, thinking it would set my clothes on fire. I stopped the car as quickly as I could, got out, and retrieved the smoldering cigarette butt. I threw it down a nearby drain, still shaken up with what unexpectedly happened. I arrived home and rushed indoors, highly aware of the pain in my thigh. But when I finally had a second to really look at the damage I had done, I saw that there was no burn mark on my trousers! The car seat was untouched, too. However, my leg hurt where the butt had landed and sat for a short while. I carefully pulled my trousers down to take a look. All that could be seen was a tiny bruise the size of the butt. After calming down, I eventually shrugged the whole thing off as one of those unexplained experiences again.

Another time, on a hot summer's day, I was lounging on some patio furniture, reading a magazine. The back of the high-back lounge chair faced the sun. After a while, I finished my magazine and decided to get up to go make tea. That's when my children noticed I had a large sunburn on my back. *Huh? How can that be? My back had been resting against the lounge chair the whole time!* I thought incredulously. I knew that the sun hadn't touched me. However, the big sunburn proved otherwise. Again, it was another unexplained moment.

These moments happen from time to time. They get my attention because they are physically different. At the same time, they are prime examples of how the afterlife body has more access past our flesh and bones. We all have so many different sides, so many different facets, and folds of who we really are. The unexplained experiences that we have depend on what we allow ourselves to see. Experiences, at times, may not make much sense, but we eventually piece them together, creating mental and physical connections, and then they become clear. It all links up like the people cutouts I learned how to make in my former art class. Everything in life is simple when we are aware and understand. It all gets easier the more we open up and see for ourselves. Is life more than the experiences of earth? I will leave the answer to that question up to you to decide.

∞

NINETEEN

From Both Sides of the Fence

The communication abilities between our physical and afterlife bodies are complex and highly efficient. Information comes through and is mixed with our experiences and the wisdom we collect while in our earthly bodies. I call this the three-way link. People usually think that all information only comes via the spirit world. Yes, the spirit world is overly guiding all the information received by a medium, but that information is mixed with the medium's own wisdom, experiences, and knowledge.

Try to imagine a universal flowing river and/or sea. All of our energies of our earthly bodies and afterlife bodies co-exist. This creates a universal sea of knowledge, thoughts, feelings, and experiences. This is also why I am able to do readings for people from different countries, over the phone, or by e-mail with no pictures or physical voices attached to the reading. Participants' vibrations are in the universal frequency mix that I can tune in to, kind of like when we tune in to a particular radio station.

Basically, I sit empty until I start to write or just type away. This action is guided by the thoughts I receive and also by the earthly experiences I have. The two complement one another. In fact, we can't have one without the other as they cannot be separated. (Separation only happens when we leave our physical bodies for other life experiences back in our real bodies in the afterlife.) The frequencies I receive, however, are different than my brainwaves. Those are where negativity, fear, and worry are stored, which could get in the way of truth.

Although these thoughts flow through me from the afterlife, they are mixed with my knowledge, wisdom, and experiences. We cannot deny one from the other two. Furthermore, remember that our two bodies are a package. Our packages are regulated with trust, which makes a balance of communication via both bodies. We all may have a physical earthly body, but we are, in truth, spiritual beings having earthly experiences. This is also why we sometimes feel like we have two voices—our physical voice and our inner voice.

Our inner voice, or higher voice as it is called by the spiritual movement, is the little voice inside our tummies. It is the voice from our real bodies, the one we use in the afterlife. Of course, we all know we have our other voice we use to communicate with by using our mouths. Our higher voice always speaks in thought because this is how we *really* communicate; it is the reason we tend to think most of the day. Try to sit in traffic and not think about anything. It's nearly impossible to do. And while we think in silence, the afterlife picks up all of those thoughts.

Our thoughts are feelings that mediums have the ability to tune in to. Of course, we have privacy and tuning in to others' thoughts is only done with their permission, or unless someone has asked for help without specifying help from either side of the fence. This is where our loved ones often come in who have passed on. They guide us in subconsciously figuring out problems or even arranging it so that we meet up with the right type of medium to help and guide us as we want.

Here's another story. One day, I was at the grocery store. I got a cart and started shopping, as usual. While in the fruits and vegetables department, I briefly left my cart by the bananas to go get some apples. When I returned to my cart, I noticed that some of my items were missing. Additionally, there were a lot of items in the cart that I had not picked up.

Bemused, I looked up. A woman was standing next to me, gathering various items. When she saw me near the cart, she suddenly said, "Hey, that's my cart!" I told her that she was mistaken and showed her that I already had a few items in it. That's when she looked at her actual cart and realized that we had accidentally switched. We both stood there, laughing. We knew we had not moved each other's items or switched carts; we had only left our carts for a couple of minutes. Apologizing with big smiles, we put our items back into our respective carts. I told her I wouldn't be surprised if a spirit person had caused the mix up, adding that I was a medium. The woman's eyes widened. "I would really like a reading today, if you can fit me in? My mother died three days ago . . ." she said quietly. Then and there, I knew that her mother must have swapped our carts around so we would meet up!

So this is what I call a three-way link between the medium, channel, and messenger. The person wanting a reading and the loved ones in the afterlife co-exist for a truthful message—a perfect mix for communication between both sides of the fence. If I share wisdom and truth, a two-way link is used between me and my experiences and the afterlife people. Three-way links and two-way links are equally used to communicate about both sides of the fence in a co-existing life of the earthly experiences we have. Guidance is shared by the afterlife so that we learn about the many ways in which we can and are able to communicate no matter what side of the fence we are on. Remember, we are all joined, equal, and united as one.

∞

TWENTY

What Are Frequencies and Vibrations?

Look down at your hands, palms-side up. Now look closely at your thumbs. You can see all the different lines on the surface, right? These, as you know, are your own personal thumbprints. Everyone has their own unique thumbprints, and they are comparable to the personal frequencies and vibrations, or telephone lines, that we have. Our physical thumbprints are used to differentiate us from each other. The vibrations and our personal frequencies that run through our afterlife bodies, or our orbs of information, contain everything we have done, thought, felt, and experienced.

The wires of energy are similar to telephone lines and store everything on all levels. Imagine the many lines on your thumbs like the grooves of a record. The grooves store all kinds of information, even though you can't physically see it. These many lines in the frequency are what mediums tune in to in order to read personal files of people requesting a reading. This process is not body language; it is more like reading Braille. It is a process of feeling and sensing first, followed by seeing or hearing the information that is picked up.

These are basic examples on the mechanics and instructions of how tuning in works. I am able to pick up on a person's personal frequency and vibration, which tells me all about them physically. Once the frequency, or link, is picked up, the loved ones in the afterlife tune in to the same frequency and pass messages through to me via this link. The actual communication between worlds is relied on more if the physical connection is working physically blind in this way. If that is the case, the telephone example is then used.

Remember that frequencies and vibrations are always storing everything every second of the day—all desires, hopes, and wishes. In short, *everything* is connected. To simplify this further, look at the sea. Now imagine we all took a jug of water from it and then turned each jug into our own unique streams. Physically, we would associate our streams as being separate from everyone else's streams. It only feels and looks like they are separate because we forget where it all came from in the first place.

All frequencies and vibrations are connected because they ultimately came from the same source. Without these frequencies, nothing would be experienced, created, or manifested. Frequencies and vibrations are what give everything *life*. Our personal frequencies are what give us character. They are responsible for our well-being, our fears, our intentions, and even our creations. Every single one of our thoughts is logged on our personal frequencies. This is why, when we go back home (telepathy), communication and relating is so instant, received, and understood. The vibrations that carry everything about us can be seen and read by everyone in the afterlife. This is our true language, not the one we use for such a short time on earth. If you think about it, it all makes sense.

Otherwise, why would we have to learn a language on earth in the first place if it was supposed to be natural to us in the whole of life?

All I am trying to do is offer the instructions to tools we already have. This is why we hear about enlightened beings who meditate quietly on their own. It is so they can tune in to frequencies of those from the afterlife and those of themselves. They are able to concentrate on the vibrations rather than being distracted by the physical doingness going on around them in the busy world.

Frequencies and vibrations connect us all as one. However, at the same time, we are unique in the oneness of the vibrations and frequencies that make us up. We can enjoy the many life experiences in the wholeness of life. Nothing ever gets lost or stolen because of the frequencies and vibrations that hold all of us. We can never be harmed or wronged, no matter what side of the fence we may find ourselves on. We forget this because our physical bodies have nerve endings. (Notice they are called nerve *endings* because they ultimately have a stopping point in the physical body.) We are lead to believe this is all we are because we can feel physical pain in the body. Remember that the feeling part is our true language—a language that we ultimately remember when we cross over and everything becomes clear again.

∞

TWENTY-ONE

FREQUENCY CHANGE UNKNOWN

As a reminder, what I share in these pages comes from my heart, or from my afterlife body—the side that remembers. What I am about to share is sort of like an afterlife postcard, so to speak. I will offer bits and pieces of information regarding the afterlife side of the fence that I am familiar with. Let's begin . . .

We try to piece together the story of earth over the centuries by digging, researching, and piecing together information we have found over time. However, some things aren't visible to the naked (or physical) eye. We have to assume things are facts based on the information, or evidence, we gather. For example, take the dinosaurs. It is thought that they were wiped out from the earth because of a solar flare or a comet's extreme impact when it hit the earth. Furthermore, there are a lot of films and discussion forums on the meaning of 2012. We tend to be drawn to apocalyptic catastrophes and all the possibilities of major happenings because of the Mayan prophecies, or Nostradamus, or of prophecies in the bible and predictions that have been made over the years. But how do we sort out fact and fiction?

Films are great because they enact what *could* happen to the world. They are a good reminder that we should not take things for granted. Sure, materialism is good at giving us a security blanket—a proverbial blanket to hide us from what we do not want to see. But materialism, to me, is like living in a cave with all our stashes of belongings inside. These often-unnecessary things tend to make us not want to venture out of the cave, or our security boxes. We forget our purpose on the planet and become comfortable collecting objects. That is no way to live our lives.

The basic necessities that we need—food, water, and shelter—do not have a lock on them. If we did not have these things, we would not survive. Unfortunately, money plays a large role in determining whether we can have these things regularly. The tables have turned on what is now important to us. Strangely, our bodies and how we treat them are no longer on top of the list. It's money and getting ahead however we can.

Years ago, what was important to people was a healthy, nutritious diet, one rich in vegetables, protein, and fruit. People weren't always on the go. They tasted real food that had been grown naturally. Today, food is grown in half the time it used to take. Animals we use for meat are filled with growth hormones so that their bodies grow unnaturally and their legs can't carry them. They receive no natural sunlight. (We all know the importance sunlight—vitamin D—has on our overall health.)

These days, food is more about quantity, not quality. Quality is slipping away at an alarming rate. Instead, it is all about the look and quickness of food, not about the actual taste or nutritional value. It's like our taste buds have become numb over the years; we have forgotten what real food tastes like. Big food companies provide food that looks okay for us to eat. Plus, the overwhelming size of most foods these days is appealing. But where are the advertisements and warning labels that say what is inside these things and how unhealthy they really are for our precious bodies?

Our overall nutrition is poor because of the foods we are consuming on a daily basis. It is no wonder why pharmaceutical companies offer so many tablets for the new viruses that we now have. When I was a kid, we just had illnesses like chicken pox, mumps and measles, earaches, and sore throats. I have noticed how everything is called and labeled a "virus" ever since having kids of my own. We are experiencing new symptoms and illnesses we are unfamiliar with. Perhaps, a big clue to this mystery starts with the food that we eat.

Our meddling with nature is what causes all of these unnatural side effects in the animals we kill for food. These side effects are causing widespread illness and suffering not only to ourselves but to the animals, too. Remember, what we put in our bodies has to come out. We are all paying out a lot of money because our health and well-being are deteriorating. It doesn't have to be this way if we choose to be mindful of what we eat.

Our well-being is determined by the actual content and quality of products we ingest. Why do we ignore the content and quality of what we put into our mouths? Why do we not think about the nasty side effects that are responsible for giving us a lot of the ailments we have today? Education plays a big part; most of us are uneducated or misinformed. The education system does not teach our children about nutritional value of foods. At the same time, it goes on about obesity. These are double standards, don't you think?

I used to be obsessed about staying thin. From the age of four, I had it in my head that my mother died from being overweight. On a physical level, this was the only explanation I had as to why she passed away. I spent the rest of my years up until just recently doing anything within my power to stay thin. Just recently, I gave up smoking. Quitting cigarettes gave me my taste buds back! I gave up cigarettes for a number of reasons. One of them was because my best friend died of lung cancer at forty-eight years old. Furthermore, most of my family members have died at young ages; genetics made our lungs not very strong.

Now that I am in my forties, my attention and focus have changed. I am more focused on what's *inside* my body rather than what's on the outside. I may be bigger than I used to be, but the changes I have noticed have been amazing. In fact, it has felt like going through puberty all over again! When I began changing what I put inside of my body, I began to see physical changes. The hair on my head is in better condition, and my nails are stronger, too. This shows that by what we put inside our bodies affects the overall condition of our physical appearance, as well as how we feel internally. My body now works how it should have worked ages ago. Well, better late than never, right?

This is all food for thought (no pun intended). While we are on the earth, we should try to grow physically and mentally as much as we can. Eating organically, drinking water, and being aware of what we put into our bodies will make us much healthier in the long run. Who knows when we will learn to leave nature alone and let it do what it has always done *naturally?* Generations gone by would never eat what we buy and consume these days. They were educated and knew about quality before quantity; they had priorities when it came to nutrition, time, patience, and nurturing. It was never about fast food or quick money turnover. There were no production lines. They knew the natural cycle of life and knew that it should not be rushed. Meanwhile, we continue to buy our illnesses and then the medicines to cure them. When will we learn?

All of this touches on frequencies within the food chains and how they affect our precious bodies on the inside—the place we do not give much time, thought, or energy to because we tend to think in an "out of sight, out of mind" way. If it don't hurt, its okay. We only start to pay attention when we feel physical pain or suddenly need hospital care. If we focus on being good to our bodies before bad things start to happen, we'll be healthier longer and we'll save a heck of a lot of money at the same time!

All the layers of life have a frequency and a vibration. This brings me back to the galaxy. It's strange to think that the truth lies where our physical eyes cannot see. We are so used to being governed by what has been in the *past*. These experiences tend to govern our future and overall outlook of life. But if I were to say that this way of looking at things is not a sure thing—after all, magnets can attract and repel each other and also connect if we just flip them over—how would you react? The bottom line is that listening is the key. If we actually listened to our bodies, we would then know what would benefit them and serve them well. Listening to the frequencies has given scientists their graphs and logs about the condition of the planet earth, as well as past, present, and future predictions. This information comes from the physical side of the fence.

The afterlife side of the fence is a little different. Say the earth is tuned in to a particular frequency. This frequency is what everyone then uses to communicate with each other. They use it for electronic equipment, satellite navigational systems, plane navigation, etc. Basically, everything that uses electricity uses this frequency. Keep in mind that *we* are also an electrical frequency. So are all the animals and plants that live around us. For years, we are happy tuning in to and using this frequency; it serves us well and does its purpose. However, electrical frequencies within the universe "shed" their particles over time. These particles then get collected up or are destroyed in the atmosphere. This shedding goes on throughout the cycles and systems. I call them "recycling cycles."

Like our skin, a new layer of frequency particles always appears on the surface. This means that the surface looks as if nothing has changed. It looks like nothing has been going on behind the scenes, or underneath, at all. Of course, this is far from what is actually going on. Have you ever noticed when you tune in to a radio station that if you do not get the right frequency, it goes all crackly and sometimes you can hear two stations at once? It does not take a lot to knock out the frequency. Sometimes we must adjust the knob or go back and forth between frequencies just so; this is called fine-tuning.

The big hype at the moment is about 2012 and natural disasters. Earth's natural disasters have happened since the world began. In fact, these occurrences are the earth's way of cleansing and shedding layers. It's kind of like the female reproduction cycle. The earth clears itself out and starts new life, shedding old matter from time to time. Scientists make records of when these things happen, hoping to make sense of it all or prevent future natural disasters from happening.

The use and understanding of frequencies and vibrations is our future. In fact, it always has been. Frequencies tell a story and send messages that help guide us in life. Frequencies have the ability to heal, feed, and nurture our bodies as a whole. This is the magic of life. Why is it, then, that we come along and try to destroy a cycle that has been around longer than us? Animals will never die out; they know how to live with the cycles of life. More importantly, they respect the earth. Humans will die first unless they remember these truths. We need to pay attention to the various cycles and frequencies and respect them, too. We forget these truths because materialism gets in the way. So does greed. It does not matter how many animals are killed in all of our meddling, animals will always survive. Why? Their natural cycle within them has not changed. *We* have changed.

It's really all about balance, common sense, and respect—morals that are not high on our list of priorities. We seem to all want a quick fix. We all want to make a quick buck. Life is not about being quick; this is why we have seasons and cycles. They are put in place so that we can learn about them and understand them. If everything was supposed to happen so quickly, how would we be able to learn? It is all about connection and working with the different frequencies of life. When things aren't aligned properly, chaos can happen—like a natural disaster. We are constantly living in a world of fine tuning frequencies. This is why we sometimes see strange weather patterns. When these things happen, it's more likely the frequency that has been tampered with.

Everyone is sensing change in some way or other. We look to the bible for clues, the symbols of ancient past, the symbols of the masons, the distant messages of predictions, and the history of life and all its natural disasters. But most of us are all still looking in the past for the answers; we are looking *backwards* to go forward. Think about the Egyptian pyramids for a minute. They point upwards, do they not? They do not point backwards or sideways, or even forward. They point upwards for a reason because the answers are within and without—an alignment of the cycles of life. We need to look for answers in the now and then be proactive.

Causes and Effects

Frequency changes are occurring all the time. But the effects are so subtle that they only get noticed when the eyes see a big change. We will always have earthquakes, tidal waves, hurricanes, tremors, and other the natural disasters. These are part of the natural life's cycle. The only difference is that we still have not learned how to live with these cycles on earth. We think we are entitled to owning pieces of the earth, which is why we have wars.

Our frequencies are changing and evolving to adapt to the future. So far, our frequencies have served their purpose. But the memory, so to speak, of what has been so far is now filled up. It's time for a new frequency in which to have new life experiences with. The transition into the new frequency will not be the cause of apocalyptic happenings; any apocalyptic occurrences are a side effect from the last frequency we used, as well as from our meddling with it.

The earth knows what it needs to do in order to survive. The natural cycle of life is the power of all life, and that's what we come from. Yes, we may notice some causes and effects in the cleaning up process while the transition into a new frequency occurs. But this will be like a clean slate, or starting on a new page. This is also why no bible, prophecies, predictions, or even the Mayans know what is to come. History has not written this new chapter yet. We are all making a new history now—one that cannot be found in old texts or history files. It is life emerging on its own terms. The whole story will soon be remembered. We have all just been too preoccupied to see it.

People wear masks in Egypt, not to cover their faces but to give us many clues about the cycles and patterns of life. We just forget what the messages mean and make them up. We've made them more complicated through our teachings than what they really are. The truth is simple, but that does not make for a good read. It would not carry much power in which to use to control people. Life and its cycle will always carry on until the way in which we live now will become a distant memory—an alien way in which to live. It will be discussed and documented in museums of the future, teaching the new children of the earth how *not* to live by our example.

We can have meaningful lives full of well-being if we focus on content and quality. We also need to slow down and do what's best for the earth. But all of this is for us to decide. We have the power to use our personal frequencies and the frequency of life to embrace change. Looking back does not hold the key. We need to use our keys in the ways that benefit us on the inside. Again, our keys are our connection to life in the unknown.

∞

TWENTY-TWO

Clutter Money

We all know the classic word used by most children is "*Why?*" They often use it as they learn about the world and question the way in which adults live. Children do not accept everything they see, which is why they ask so many questions in the first place. There should be no shame in using the word. In fact, it enables us to question things and not accept everything we are told.

I have always thought that children have more sense than adults. When they are young and innocent, they are still unchanged and influenced by materialism, greed, and the many negative layers of falseness. They don't yet know what lying is. They question the world in which we live, always asking, "Why?"

Generations pass down only what they know by encouraging children to live a life under the illusion that adults have already put in place. As adults, we want children to fit in accept the ways of the world as we know them. We discourage them from asking questions. Perhaps, sometimes, we are afraid that we won't know all of the answers. We are too busy playing out the illusion—acting out what or who we think we should be to the world—and teaching our children to follow in our footsteps rather than being ourselves and allowing the kids to simply be kids.

This innocent illusion game that we teach to our children is what's to blame for the lack of ability to speak the truth of our thoughts, feelings, and observations. This game creates so many problems and difficulties because it leads to the biggest plague of all: fear. This secret code is so subtle yet so ingrained in our minds. And unfortunately, it affects everyone. It always comes back to fear, which stems from our innocent generational pass down—a history of control through fear and threats, which still create fear, no matter how we look at anything or how decisions are made by anyone. Fear will always be the ruling factor in everything we do. The illusion of fear controls us. It discourages us to be the individuals we are supposed to be.

Children don't know a lot when they are young; it is sometimes difficult for them to distinguish right from wrong. They are not listened to and are not taken seriously. But maybe they hold the secrets to our freedom in life? Maybe we could learn a lot by their essence and how they express themselves without any fear? Adults spend a lot of time trying to recapture their youth, but maybe we are missing the key here? Perhaps we *should* listen to what children have to say.

As children grow up, the secret of the self has to be numbed and not used so that they can forget, like us. The system does not want individual-minded adults in the world; they would damage the controlled world we have spent so long trying to create. These folks would pose a threat to the rest of us. This is why we try to make children conform to what we know. We want them to accept how things are without questions. If they obey us, we can carry on controlling the world and the fearful adults. It's a careful plan that was established centuries ago. We live in a highly manipulated way.

Parents should be thankful for their children's questions; it shows they have an interest in the world. We should encourage them to keep their minds when the illusion of history past encourages us to lose it. We should communicate by discussing questions and answers until our children feel they have firm grasps on whatever topics they're interested in. In fact, we should ask questions ourselves! Are we followers or leaders? If we are followers, what will we do to change that? Personally, I have chosen to be a leader and go against the grain. Schools and the adult world don't like people like me. I ask too many questions. I refuse to be told to keep quiet. Does this remind you of something? It reminds me of being a child! So, are adults *really* adults? Either way, I will never lose my childlike spirit of questioning.

Have you ever questioned anything "too much"? Has anyone ever tried to shush you because you wanted to find out more about something? Practice having no fear, be brave, and speak and feel your own truth. Free yourself from the illusion bubble created to take all your power away from you in order to make you forget who you are and why you are here. Hold onto *you* no matter how small a part that feels at times. It's not our faults that we have innocently given parts of ourselves up as children, and as adults it's never too late to claim those parts back!

It's funny how we tend to accept most things in life, even when they don't seem okay. When our little voices speak out, we should *listen*. Our gut feelings are usually right. Imagine the changes we could make in the world if everyone just started speaking out—if everyone acted on their inner voices and weren't afraid . . .

I had a nagging question a few years back. I wondered why we drive ourselves crazy and stress ourselves out just to make what I refer to as "clutter money." I looked at all the people who lived near me—everyone rushing around, living to work so that they could pay for their homes. But *why?* Why do house prices continue to go up when the actual houses don't change or improve?

Real estate seems to be the biggest moneymaker in the adult world. Furthermore, the whole real estate market seems to have the biggest amount of manipulation involved with it. It is carefully controlled so that adults do exactly as they are told by banks and the government. One of our basic necessities is shelter; we all need a roof over our heads. The government takes any other form of housing away by enforcing planning permissions. We have no other choice than to turn fearful that we won't have shelter. We accept the fact that we have to live to work in order to make payments on houses that already cost too much money. We have limited freedom all in the name of clutter money.

We buy, we sell, we need, and we have, all quick, all now. But haven't we already realized that we never actually *own* anything? The deeds we keep locked up in our safes are all part of the security illusion trap. Everything is loaned to us, or rented out, using clutter money. This illusion is hidden by power and control over all of us. Have fun with observing the world and with what we spend our money on. But remember, look after *you*, first and foremost; the clutter money will always look after itself.

∞

TWENTY-THREE

Our Subconscious Minds

As you can see from the previous chapter, our lives are governed by a clever, subtle plan. It's like slow hypnosis. Seeds of manipulation are carefully planted into our minds through advertising and the media. Calculated advertisements tell us what we need and want using subliminal messages. We all thought the invention of technology, and more specifically, the Internet, was our biggest electronic advancement. In some ways, the answer is yes. It is much easier and faster to chat with someone in another country than it was before computers and cell phones. But there is also a flipside to all of this. Our technological advances are numbing our brains, making them dormant. We are becoming more and more reliant on the systems we have in place.

We all go shopping, right? Have you ever noticed that sales clerks are becoming much more reliant on computers to think and do the actual work for them? Look for yourself and see how dependant people truly are. It is as if the computers are a higher power and not to be questioned; they must be accurate all the time, right? No, this is not always the case at all.

Practically our entire banking system, for example, and our advancement in technology, in general, has allowed us to get lazy. We let machines and computers do everything for us. We have lost the human brainpower to solve problems by actually working things out ourselves. Does this sound safe to you? It's like we are all turning into robots! How many times have we all been put on hold on the phone, or told to wait a few minutes at a store because "the system is down"? (Yet, it still takes three days for a check to clear in a bank. Not much has changed there!)

We are fed messages every day on what to wear, what to eat, what to buy, what new gadgets to have, etc. We live in a world full of tempting clutter goods to clutter up our homes so that we can't even move in them. We become so entertained by the latest gadgets that we do not even talk to each other anymore. We are led to believe it's all in good fun, but there is a price to pay. That price is giving ourselves and our minds away to the system the governments and dictators have created.

We all see the devastating effects natural disasters have on people in different parts of the world—take Haiti, for example. A lot of times, natural disasters seem to happen to countries that don't have a lot in the first place. What they do have, however, are independent life skills; these people are used to surviving with very little. Just because we live comfortably in the Western World doesn't mean this could not happen to us. How would people of today survive a disaster in the Western World? We are so used to having and relying on our materialistic possessions.

We need to be aware of our everyday actions and habits. If we are not aware of ourselves, how are we going to be aware of the system and how it uses our subconscious minds to mould us into how it really wants us to live? We are all so busy and preoccupied with all of our gadgets that we take our minds off the whole picture—of what *really* matters.

I would not be surprised if the next world war is a human one, not a country-to-country war. How would anyone survive such a disaster? Not many teenagers know how to cook or sew these days. Instead, kids focus on their computers and electronic game skills. They laugh at adults for being a bit slow. Where does common sense fit into these electronic games? This is what worries me. *Skills* are needed to be remembered and passed down to teach our young how to cook and sew—the basics. Knowing the basics allows them to be able to adapt to any situation they may find themselves in.

Recently, my family has gone backwards, you could say, in order to go forward. We have planted many fruit trees, herbs, and nut trees. Our food shopping has changed; I try to buy natural foods as much as possible. I often cook our meals from scratch—the old-fashioned way, I suppose. I boil all my meat rather than roast it. I could go on and on but the bottom line is that the benefits have been adding up for my family. We are making positive and healthy life changes.

Making small lifestyle changes really does add up. Hopefully, these pages will help awaken everyone to the illusions of life. If a disaster happened, how would *you* manage? How would you survive with no electricity or water? If you can answer these questions, then you are awake. Good for you! Our subconscious minds are quietly being manipulated but are you actively conscious of what is going on?

Simply put, all the money circulating in the world just passes from one hand to another. It is all borrowed from the public—us. The banks own nothing and have no money. Instead, they play with ours. This is the way it has always been. We are just not told the truth. If banks had all this money, why can we only withdraw small amounts? If we ever want to take out more than a few thousand dollars, we have to give them notice so that they can borrow it from somewhere else before giving it to us.

If a natural disaster *did* happen in the Western World, and everyone wanted to take their money out of the banks all at once, I am sorry to tell you that it would not exist. None of us would get it. Why? It doesn't physically exist—just the numbers do. The banks figure that people will always want to keep their money—or should I say, calculated numbers—in there, so the few who do take money out is such a small number compared to what is in the actual system. Banks juggle around the few thousand dollars they really do have in their offices and gain interest off of us, thus allowing them to play and juggle even more.

I would love to see the day when the whole population went to the banks and everyone demanded that their money be withdrawn at the same time. I know what would happen. The truth would then be revealed and the banks and all the system's infrastructure would collapse just like the Berlin Wall. Well, this would collapse the illusion that the banks have so conveniently created so that we live under their rules and control.

This is the power of illusion and money and its control over us. We are being so blinded by money and what it can buy us that it hides the truth that has been going on for hundreds of years. We buy houses that we will never *really* own. The government doesn't own them, either. Who does? Our planet does. Remember, everything we think we own has been *given to* us to make things for us to live in while we have our life experiences here. There was never any mention about a price tag. In the beginning, everything was (and should still be) free.

The physical structure on the land made from materials of the land is not ours to own, but to share—otherwise we would take our houses with us when we go to the afterlife. The moral of the story here is people come and go but the houses and all the stuff we play with stays with the earth. There may come a time when Mother Earth wants to reclaim some of her materials back. The truth is that the earth owns everything. It is all just loaned out to us to use freely. We have put price tags on these things as well as on our freedom, thus putting price tags on our minds, too.

How do you see the world and the things you use? What do you *own?* How much money do you think you really have? Enjoy finding out your own truths. I hope you have enjoyed reading about mine.

∞

TWENTY-FOUR

RESISTANCE OF CHOICES

Have you ever heard someone say, "If only I could turn back the hands of time . . ."? We have all said something similar to this at some point in our lives. Some of these feelings may have been about regrets. Some may have been about wishful thinking. Others may have been about holding on and not letting go. Some could have been about disbelief. Whatever they're about, they all have one thing in common: They are words of acknowledgement about a situation, a crisis, or circumstances that are now out of our control.

These feelings are layers of absorbing an impacting situation that gets our total attention. Ultimately, we want to accept what happened, whatever it was, so that we can let go and move on. Life is all about making choices and the causes and effects our decisions create. We are constantly being presented with multi-layered possibilities.

This is why words such as "right" or "wrong" are so misleading. We feel like we are living on a tightrope that we have to balance on, and we use all of our might to stay on top of everything. The real tightrope of life is so wide that it's immeasurable. It is so big that physical eyes cannot see it. Look outside and tell me that you can see what air looks like. The only time we have a slight clue is when the wind blows the leaves on the trees, -or when we hear it howl. Air just is. It is not seen for what it is; it is only seen for what it can do. Again, we have the physical *doing* word. The afterlife, on the other hand, is simply *being* what it *is*. Words that are *doing* words are physical connections to the physical world. Being words are just *is* words. They do not need to *do* to *be*.

This is where the battle of the wills comes in. We say or hear things like, "Oh, I do wish so-and-so had taken my advice . . ." or "If only they had listened and took the other route home . . ." *Listening* is the key word here. Do we listen to the advice of others or listen to ourselves? After all, we came here to go on our own journeys using our own personal maps of experiences. I am with myself for all eternity regardless of my age, gender, color, creed, labels, etc. I should know me better than anyone else! How would anyone else know what I want to experience?

Our physical bodies may pull us in different directions and be influenced from time to time, but deep down our souls—our afterlife bodies—hold the keys of what we really want to experience, even if physically we do not know. This is where internal guidance comes into play, or gut feelings. These moments help us remember what's on our personal maps. If we get lost en route and find ourselves at dead ends, or going around in circles with no end in sight, guidance gives us a gentle hand to find a new route altogether; it helps put us back on the right path.

When I reached my late thirties, I wasn't sure what I wanted to do next in my life. I had thought about going back to college, out of curiosity, because I was in the process of writing a book about being an orphan. Growing up, I had been told by professionals that

I was "uneducatable." Translation: *Give up on her. She is a lost cause—completely hopeless*. Unfortunately, this label stuck with me for many years. At the same time, the little voice inside of me said, *If only people had given me a chance. If only they could see past my childhood experiences, the ones that limited me in my learning abilities because survival, back then, was more important in my home life*. Something always has to give under challenging situations, right?

I wanted to go back to college just to see what my learning capabilities were. I wanted to see for myself whether this label really belonged to me. At the time, I was working part-time doing readings in a local shop. I noticed the shop also provided Indian Head massage services. The word "Indian" made me curious more than anything because it was a word that I was familiar with—because of my Indian guide, Ramini. I thought about it for a few days until I gathered enough courage to make an appointment at the college for an interview. I was ready to enroll.

What am I doing? Why am I doing this? What do I want to learn this for? I asked myself in a mini panic on the day of the interview. I thought it would be good to know about the anatomy and physiology. I was curious to learn more about our physical body parts and what they do. During readings, the physical body parts would come up from time to time and I would not know what they were or what they did. I hoped the person receiving the message would know.

I walked to the college, reluctantly dragging my heels. It felt like I was being dragged by my afterlife body ear by my afterlife guide. (This was true.) At the interview, my first hurdle came. "This is a level three diploma course," the counselor said. "The course work is done by computer. It is not handwritten."

Oh, no! I thought. *I am not sure this is for me. It sounds well out of my depth. I have never used a computer in my life! Should I just walk out or should I take a leap of faith and sign up for the course?* My fears of inadequacy and remembering how I had been labeled as "uneducatable" made me want to run away. However, I still felt pinned down by the afterlife guidance around me. So I took a deep breath and signed up for the course, the unknown. The history of my childhood haunted my thoughts of what was to come, but I willed myself not to succumb to fear.

In the next two weeks, I had to get a computer, figure out how to set it up, and then actually use it. The big day arrived of my first lesson. We all introduced ourselves and listened to the professor for the next three hours. Leaving class, I excitedly clutched my first assignment that was due the following week. This experience was a massive challenge. But it was a challenge I wanted to face so I could finally have a true understanding of what my learning capabilities were. It was a challenge I was more than up for!

The year's course came and went. I had handed all my assignments and case studies in on time. All that was left was our final exam. When that was over, I had nothing else to do but go home and wait for the results. Had I passed? Had I failed? It felt like throwing a coin up in the air and waiting to see if it landed on heads or tails.

The results finally came back. The professor looked at me and smiled. "I am pleased you have passed with distinction!" she said, holding my exam in her hands.

I was shocked. "Really?" I replied. "Are you sure?"

"Yes, you have. Look," she said, handing the exam to me.

Indeed, I had proved that I was "educatable." That negative label did not belong to me. I had achieved and faced what I needed to experience to find out what I was capable of when my life's earlier experiences had not given me the chance. I suddenly felt like I could face the world with all the pieces of me that had been ripped up. This new experience helped put all those bits and pieces back together.

Had I not taken a chance on myself, I would never have known what I was capable of. That day was a battle of the wills from both sides of the fence. And although I was encouraged with a helping hand from Ramini, knowing I was not walking into that college on my own was a great comfort in itself. But ultimately, it was still up to me with my own free will and choice on whether I wanted to face my fears of the past. I chose to walk through the door, and I came out the other side feeling better than when I first walked in. It was not easy and took a lot of hard work, and many hours of studying. But it was worth it just to have a passing grade—and one with distinction at that!—and to know I was smart after all.

Admittedly, my *weak* strengths did shine at times during that course. In fact, they made the professor laugh many times, but laughter is not a crime, is it? Laughter is life. I have never been a very good artist. At one point during the course, we had to draw muscles and parts of the body. Apparently, one of my drawings looked more like the shape of a specific male organ. I can't help the fact that the particular muscle we were supposed to draw had a similar shape! Oh well. Doing our best, no matter how funny or embarrassing something may end up being, is all that counts. To me, the laughs were an added bonus.

That day I nearly resisted a new experience for many layered reasons. Our fears can get in the way of opening up new doors that may lead to exciting new experiences. By being brave enough to open just one leads then to another and so on. Guidance is helpful in situations like this, when we feel unsure of ourselves because of something new or different, when it is just guidance and not control. Guidance is not the same thing as empowerment or taking over someone else's life. If that were the case, we may as well step inside someone else's life and live it for them.

Remember that our maps are personal and unique to us. They will not be the same maps as anyone else's. The roads on our maps may pass one another at any given time. They have the ability to weave in and out with each other. Our maps are our afterlife fingerprints. But this is where we get confused between our own maps and the maps of others—like our children's, for example. I have always told my children that I am no different than them; I am just older in years. I tell them that they do not owe me for anything and vice versa. Furthermore, I have thanked them for choosing me to be their mother and assured them that I will guide them and teach them everything I know. At the same time, I knew that they would equally teach me things.

I am a vessel for my children to have their earthly experiences. I will always love and cherish them but in the space of freedom. Love between us is like an elastic band—a bond that never gets broken unless the love is not felt anymore and becomes disconnected. In freedom, our children are loved so we equally have space to experience life in love. Like pillars, they stand strong knowing love never ends no matter where life's experiences take us. I do not own my children. I love them. Love is home, a feeling, a knowing, one in which we all belong and are connected if we so desire to be.

Have you ever felt pulled in various directions by many people because of their expectations of you? (This can happen when we have kids!) When it does happen, we sometimes forget that we have our own lives to live. We cannot always be someone else's servant or entertainer. It is unhealthy to constantly have others "piggybacking" off of us. This is called codependency. Sometimes, love comes in different forms—especially when one of the people in a relationship becomes too codependent on the other person. We feel hurt or guilty when we have to be cruel to be kind. But we must always be honest and face the truth, rather than feeding a dependent person.

It is important to change patterns that no longer serve anyone involved in an experience. This change can be scary because it is the unknown; no one likes the word "no." No is considered bad or wrong, depending on how we look at it. However, the word no can actually be a lifeline or a friend in times of change. Always saying yes to please people may not help them get on their own two feet; it can also stress *us* out. We need to keep our personal limits in mind before we say yes to something. A gentle but firm no can actually help more than just giving in to something. I call these the "plasters of life." They are used to cover up certain things—quick fixes to save time.

As adults, we think we have been around long enough to know everything. We are lead to believe that because we are of a certain age that we have all the wisdom in the world. Underneath, however, we are all still children. It doesn't matter how young or old we are. We still sometimes feel scared, overwhelmed, overworked, misunderstood, taken for granted, or limited with our circumstances. We still sometimes feel lost, confused, trapped, unloved, or unlovable. In the end, it's all about owning up to who we are regardless of our ages.

Numbers, or our ages, simply reflect how long our earthly experiences have been occurring for. Experience is measured not by numbers but by the depths of our hearts and our essence. Just because our birthdays say we are sixty-five years old, for example, does not mean anymore than that. Our beingness does not need a number associated with it because it just is. Sometimes, this is what causes the conflict between the real us and our physical ages.

Ability is governed by a number, but why? Who is to say that as soon as we reach a certain age we can do certain things or that we must stop doing certain things? I would like to gently remind everyone that we are all in the big playground of life together, regardless of our numbers in any shape or form. Numbers are grades but they do not reflect a person's abilities or capabilities. How a person feels and his or her attitude is what is important. Sometimes, what we feel we can't do one day is perfectly manageable another day.

Remember, real life has no end or beginning; life is about continuation and moving on to the next experience. Things change and evolve all the time, and we are continually learning life skills because of this. But if we do not actually master things, who gives anyone the right to grade people and what they do? We should only be able to judge ourselves. Deep down, we know what our abilities and limits are.

Our physical sides compete with other people from the same side of the fence. We fight because we believe that we are entitled to whatever we want. We are greedy for money and materialistic goods. Confusion causes the resistance of choices—the battle of the physical side of our will. Remember, our physical eyes let us only see from the physical side. We only *think* we see and know everything. We tend to be self-centered and don't understand why people do not take our advice or listen to us.

All the signposts remind us that there are always two sides to every story: one we can physically see and one we can't unless we use our afterlife eyes to see the whole picture. Something may physically look right, but our afterlife maps are the real plans. Certain experiences are chosen not just for the benefit of ourselves, but to also sometimes benefit others who have asked to experience something. They offer themselves to take part in an experience to aid someone else. We only believe that we are separate and not working as a team—when really we are. Remember, we are all part of the picture of life, weaving together life's experiences collectively. *Together*, we all learn what we have asked for, according to our personal maps of life.

Through the eyes of the afterlife, the whole makes more sense and shows its real depth and meaning. Physically, we only get half of the story—half of the picture. We then judge experiences and grade them as good, bad, horrible, traumatic, etc. We forget that behind the scenes of physical life lie great plans for us. These plans are our life maps. They show us the whole picture that we are experiencing, something we fully understand in the great scheme of things. This picture does not need class, judgment, or measurement of worth because everything is known and so are the reasons why. There is no confusion and no regrets. Some of our experiences are for us to learn more; some of our experiences are offerings of gifts to give others who may need a helping hand. Nothing is wasted and whatever we are left with is always a gift for us to use—a gift in the eyes of the afterlife body, a judgment in the eyes of the physical.

No experience—past, present, or future—has the ability to harm the wholeness of who we are. Only our judgment of the experience gives it the power to have a meaning. The true meaning will always be experienced in a benefit, never a loss. This perception is personal, depending on what side of the fence we are observing life from. Remember, our personal free will and choice gives us freedom to feel and believe anything we want to believe.

Life will always have many layers within the many experiences that we want to have. Our reactions to such experiences depend on the resistance we put up against changes that occur around us all the time. Nothing ever stays still. Life is a revolving door into many rooms. We have the option to see experiences either as a gift or as a judgment. How we choose to feel about any given experience rests in our own hands.

∞

TWENTY-FIVE

Meet You Halfway

Do you remember your first day at elementary school? Do you remember walking through the big gates and up the path toward the school? Your first taste of the unknown! How frightening did that feel? One of your parents or your caretaker made sure you had your backpack and your lunch and then said, "Now I can only come this far with you because I am too big for school. You must go on your own now . . ."

"What!?" you exclaimed. "You can only come halfway with me?" Then all through the day, you wonder in the back of your mind if you're ever going to be picked up again. *Will I be forgotten about and left to stay here forever?*

Those first moments of the unknown and the first taste of meeting someone only halfway can feel like a load of butterflies in our tummies. These feelings stay throughout our lifetimes and have the ability to reappear from time to time whenever the unknown is suddenly faced again. But wouldn't these first experiences be so much easier if we understood the whole process and that doing things on our own helps build our character, showing us that we don't always need to hold someone's hand to get things done in life?

When we don't understand a process but are told we need to partake in it, we can feel as if we are all alone and have to face everything on our own. We are told to be brave, but what if we are not feeling brave? We are looked at as if we have something wrong with us for feeling a certain way. However, truth be known, it is not the feeling of not being brave that is the problem here. The problem lies with the person who sees it and does not know how to handle his or her feelings. Instead, we try to brush them off or barter with things. Or we use bribes. This is another example of the sticking plaster quick fix to a problem that an adult does not know how to handle. It all seems innocent but what these innocent gestures teach us is that feelings can be bought and healed by gifts. Instead, we should learn how to face *why* we feel how we are feeling.

The other way in which feelings of thought are handled and, sadly in schools by some teachers and heads of schools, to use threats as a means of bartering with children to behave. How are these methods nurturing our young and educating them about feelings? They aren't. Adults who use these methods do not fully understand the process of feelings with thoughts, or why we even have them in the first place. They make it seem as if feelings are an inconvenience, like a wasteful byproduct.

HALFWAY FEELINGS

Feelings are our hearts of our lives. They have a lot to do with our existence. In fact, feelings should be prioritized, like food and water, not treated as trash that needs to go in the recycle bin with little or no interest. Halfway feelings mean that we are only half-aware that they are there. Feelings are like minefields in life; they rest underneath our language. If our language ever creates a barrier, it is no wonder why our feelings become barriers as well.

Why is it so wrong to own what we feel? Whenever we have a headache, which is a feeling of pain, we seem to have no problem letting the people around us know about it. The same goes for if we have stomachaches. For some reason, feelings of pain are acceptable to us. Others can see its validity. Physical evidence, such as a doctor's note or a prescription, dictates that it's okay to feel things when it comes to pain. How come we can't be allowed to feel with anything else?

There are *many* layers of feelings that we feel. One main feeling because of an experience may branch off to other feelings as we try to make sense of everything. A feeling of pain can morph into a feeling of anger or sadness or both. All these stored feeling pieces that we hold in our backpacks of life can't be stored inside forever. However, a lot of us try to do that anyway, and soon we cannot see or feel what feeling belongs where.

This is how the many layers of life work with all of our senses. By sorting one feeling out, which may make the feeling pain go away, we forget that we still have the other similar associated pieces to deal with; they still need to be faced. Sometimes, we believe that we have already faced them and sorted them out because we have dealt with one feeling. We think that means all of them have been sorted out. It may *feel* like that at first until a situation triggers us and reminds us that we are still holding onto a bunch of feelings that still need to be tended to and understood. Only then can we truly accept and move on from an experience.

Recognizing how many feeling cards we are holding in our hands allows us to realize what feelings are unfinished and what feelings we can let go of. At times, we may think that because someone else is helping us or dealing with our emotions and feelings for us, our feelings or these specific experiences do not necessarily belong to us anymore; we think they aren't our own personal responsibility. We forget that these are always going to be our feelings or mapped out experiences, not those of the person we believe to be dealing with them.

When this happens, we sometimes find it a shock when certain feelings come back and bite us when we least expect them to, especially when we thought these feelings were dealt with years ago. We forget that our feelings are like an elastic band that has been stretched far away from us. At some point, it will undoubtedly ping straight back. The surprise is in the stretching part—out of sight, out of mind. Or it's more like out of reach, out of feel.

Many years ago, when I was still new at doing readings, I met a young girl who was in the afterlife. She was unable to settle and fully move on to her next life, her real life, because her earthly life still had some unfinished business to tend to. The girl had been murdered, yet her body had never been found. (The murder took place before I began working with others.) She unexpectedly visited me at home one day in my kitchen and we began communicating. Over the next two years, I grew to love the girl and get to know her like she was my own daughter. In fact, this two-year experience would be the biggest learning experience that I would ever have when it came to doing readings and helping afterlife people. I had grown up believing that everything had to be solved. I thought life was all about solving our problems. Looking back, I was so naïve. That young girl taught me so much about the work I would go on to do.

When I first met her, naturally I thought she wanted me to help solve her murder—the unfinished business of her earthly life experience. I was so wrong! It took two years of our friendship and two years after the experience to work out all the pieces. When we first started working together, I felt like I had been thrown in the deep end of a pool with no ladder or sides to climb out. I was still learning the afterlife language; it was still very new to me. The communication process was a slow one, to say the least. It took a while to fully understand the symbols and pictures that were presented to me. But the young girl was always very patient.

She shared the last details of her physical life during that four-year time span. When all was said and done, I finally had a statement of events and a rough summary of what had occurred the night she was murdered. The next step, I thought, was to officially solve the problem and find the actual murderer. I tried with all my heart and soul to crack the case and help the young girl finally be able to rest in peace, but it was no use. The entire experience made me feel like my soul was breaking in two. I felt like I had failed her. To have one's soul ache is much different from a hurting heart.

The day came when we both knew the girl was ready to let go of her physical life experience; she had done what she needed to do. But I, on the other hand, still felt like the experience was only *half* completed. Still, I reluctantly put all the pieces that we had been working with to one side and accepted that she had shared all that she needed to share with me. It was hard. I never physically liked goodbyes. And as I mentioned, I had grown very close and protective of the young girl.

She was ready to move on. We held each other's afterlife hand and walked through some fields. I felt a pang in my soul; I didn't want to say goodbye. However, I knew we would always have a connection. In the distance, we saw a half-opened door. There was a shadow around it. And as I looked through the opening, I saw how alive and how bright it was on the other side. I smiled and turned to face the girl as we let go of each other's hand. "That's the door for you to walk through, my love," I whispered to her. "I can only go halfway with you. You have to go through on your own as it is not my time yet." She looked at me, smiling back, and said nothing. I know that her smile was one of acceptance and love.

I stood still and watched as she walked ahead of me toward the door. As soon as she walked through the doorway, the door closed behind her. I exhaled slowly, knowing that she could finally rest and move on with her new life—her afterlife. I felt happy and honored to have witnessed her settling into her new life and holding her hand and walking with her halfway to the next chapter of her life. I was pleased that she chose me to use as her sounding board. Being a messenger now meant more than simply passing messages to people on earth. It meant being there to listen to afterlife people talk about their earthly life experiences. My relationship with the young girl opened up for me what being a medium meant, and how varied the work would be from both sides of the fence.

That day was one of my most treasured memories. Being a messenger offers a gift not in money but in life and what it really means. I walked away amazed at having had such an experience. To watch her move on really was like watching her be reborn into a new life experience. There was nothing sad or gloomy about it. Instead, the experience was full of love and appreciation.

Once I came back down to earth, I still only felt half-complete. The other half of me was still trying to make sense of all the pieces of information I had from the girl's earthly experience. The physical side of me felt pain in my soul. I still felt like I had somehow let her down. However, the spirit side of me knew the truth and felt at peace with what had happened. My afterlife side knew that she would not have moved on if she still felt she had unfinished business left on earth to sort out. Besides, who I am to judge whether someone else's life is unfinished or not? I realized that my uneasiness was about my feelings toward the experience and not hers. When that dawned on me, I let it go and put all the details away to a corner of my mind. I didn't place them out of sight, out of mind completely. I simply let go and trusted that although it still all didn't make sense to me, someday it would.

And it did. A few years later, the answer to all of this finally came to me. I realized that our meetings together were not about *solving* the murder mystery. It was about *listening*. All she needed from me was a friend who would listen and give her the time that she needed to sort things out on her own. She needed to tell at least one person her truth to the confusing last moments of her physical life—her statement of events. That was all she needed from me in order to finally rest. She wanted to have a voice so she could speak her own truth for herself . . . and no one else.

She saw the bigger picture and knew that if things changed physically, all the good work others had done as a result of her earthly life experience could potentially do more harm than good. Her family members were doing many good things because of it. Changing what they already knew would upset the good they were doing; furthermore, it wouldn't change what had happened. Sometimes it is best if things are left as they are. And that was the girl's gift to them. She knew that they would all have the answers to it all. To let go means to give.

The young girl gave me a gift of understanding. Being a messenger is not about solving problems. It is about gentle guidance to the whole and listening. By listening to her, I was able to help her move on. And by understanding what all the experience meant for both of us, I could now let go and move on, too. I was able to see how both halves of a story make a continuing picture in which life can add more and more experiences to.

Meeting halfway with another soul allows us to find out about many things, even if it is many years later when the experience makes more sense. The truth is the truth even if the physical side cannot see it clearly because the afterlife half makes no sense. Trust me, it will all piece together one day. It doesn't matter what side of life we are on. We are all connected and everything will always connect back to us eventually. We need to remember not to let the shells of our physical bodies hide what amazing people we truly are.

∞

TWENTY-SIX

SHADOWS OF DARKNESS, SHADOWS OF LIGHT

Our first glimpse of darkness is usually at bedtime when we are small. I remember one night, at the children's home, when we were all sent to bed. With so many kids to a room, it was oftentimes hard to fall asleep. Someone would always have a case of the giggles, usually because whoever was on the bottom bunk of the bunk beds would stretch his or her legs straight up into the metal base of the top bunk. This made whoever was lying on the top bunk to be raised up in the middle unexpectedly. Other times, we'd break out into fits of laughter whenever someone placed one hand into his or her opposite arm pit and squeeze the arm down repeatedly, causing a very loud fart sound.

Well, this particular night, we just would not go to sleep. The staff members on the evening shift got very annoyed with us. After three unsuccessful attempts to get us to close our eyes, the next visitor was not a staff member but a sister, or so we thought, based on her headdress and cross around her neck. She yelled at us in a thick Irish accent and slammed the door. (Years later, when I visited the homes to take pictures for my scrapbook, this night was mentioned. One of the staff members on duty at the time admitted that the scary nun had been her all along. She only dressed up so that we would quiet down and go to sleep!)

It's incredible what darkness can hide when the eyes can't see. We have many layers and shades of darkness—the pitch black of the night, a blinding darkness when a scarf is tied around the eyes, the nightlight in the corner of the bedroom, the candlelit room casting shadows on the walls. But we tend to refer to darkness as one blackness. We associate the dark with ghosts, graveyards, and spooky stories. Who lives in the darkest shadows? The bogeyman and the sandman, of course!

But who really *is* the bogeyman? What did he look like? Was he made up of green slimy boogers? No one ever asks these kinds of questions—especially not children; they would rather not know. As a child, I believed that the tall, long shape in the corner of my bedroom that always moved toward the door was, in fact, the dreaded bogeyman. But if that was so, why did he keep moving across the same place to the door over and over again? I eventually figured it out as I get older: The bogeyman was really just the headlights of various cars driving past, shining in the bedroom as they continued on. We create our own fear in our minds based on things we do not know or understand.

Have you ever wondered why being afraid of the dark starts when we are little? We do not know *why* we are afraid of the dark, we just are! Well, it is because children who are fresh from the afterlife world are used to a life of light. They are simply used to living in light; darkness is not part of their past lives (unless they have wished it to be, or believe it to be). Naturally, arriving to earth is a bit of a shock to their afterlife body halves. That side of the body remembers the light and warmth. The feeling and experience of darkness is the opposite of what they have been used to. This takes a lot of adjustment, sometimes years. But because babies and children do not remember *why* the dark is strange to them physically, they have to find some other reason for feeling scared in their minds to make sense of it all.

This is where the bogeyman comes into play; he makes the most sense. It is not because the physical eyes can't see; our minds tell us to believe stories like this. Most adults don't admit they are scared of the dark. This just happens to children, blamed on vivid imaginations because, truth be known, *no one* remembers. Only the soul's memory in the afterlife body does. The soul knows and remembers a life where darkness is not known unless someone wants to have a life lived within the dark. The light in the afterlife is reenergizing, healing, calming, soothing, loving, and relaxing all at the same time. Light is in everything.

This is why most of us enjoy sunbathing under the sun's warm rays. We instantly feel relaxed and calm—a state the afterlife body feels all the time when in the afterlife life. Knowing this, we can only imagine what a shock it is for people who come to earth for the first time to feel what cold and darkness are like! This is why babies scream and why plants always turn and face the light when potted on windowsills. Everything in life—human beings, plants, animals, and vegetables—all know this truth deep down.

Darkness could not exist without light because light creates everything. We are never completely in the dark. Try and find total darkness. It will prove to be impossible. Even at nighttime, the stars and the moon shine brightly in the sky. If we didn't have streetlights, the natural particles of the universe would still shine down. The sun is always shining no matter where we are in the world. Remember, just because our eyes do not see light does not mean it's not there.

Light is the main color and spectrum where other colors come from; therefore, darkness does not exist. It is simply a paler shade of light that our eyes see. Even blind people are still able to see shades of light. Pure darkness does not exist. Only pure light does, and it can create many different shades for us to experience and understand. We tend to accept this and carry on with our lives without questioning it.

Have you noticed something amazing about all the truths of life I talk about? They all have one thing in common which is opposite to the life experiences of earth. I will let you in on the secret that you already know. Air is something that we can't hold on to—it just is . . . life! Darkness is something that we can't hold on to—it just is. The sun is something that we can't hold on to—it just is. Light is something that we can't hold on to—it just is. And if you remember, darkness actually is the light in disguise. Basically, we have three forces of life. Light is the life force of everything. It helps to create a unity among all living things. It creates a togetherness, or a balance in all of life's cycles. We all live within the many layers, cycles, seasons, and experiences of life as one.

Everything that we physically hold on to is not real life; it is all made up of shadows—reflections of what we *believe* life to be while we're participating in our earthly experiences. The afterlife body in the light of night does not need to hold on to anything because it already knows it has everything it needs freely in life.

People, animals, and plants have come and gone in life's cycle of continuation, and the earth has fed them all. Some have been fed more easily than others. But even after all these centuries, we have remembered very little. In fact, it seems that we have forgotten more than the generations of centuries past. Why? Well, food costs money. Clothes cost money. Houses cost money. Even water costs money. Fuel and energy definitely cost money. Are you seeing a pattern here? We have created a manmade lifestyle for our physical lives. This is why materialistic goods are found in old tombs and pyramids along with the skeletons of the dead. We forget that we don't need any of these physical goods in the afterlife. The materialistic things are all for the earth and for whoever is having earthly experiences.

This is why we have wills—forms filled out and paid for to the solicitor, making it legal, according to the piece of paper, to hand down our materialistic goods to those who are still having earthly experiences. (Our real afterlife bodies have *free* will and choice—the real will of real life.) Real life is not a business; it never has been. All of the money in the world can't buy a happy heart and peace of mind. Pieces of paper, whether they are money or legal documents, are all the same. They just have different names, numbers, and labels on them. Passing around pieces of paper will not stop the cycle of life. When it's time to transition over to the other side, we will realize that we actually own nothing—and never truly did.

We are supposed to use what the earth has provided for us to use while we are here. Have you ever thought about why we have two hands? One is to give and one is to receive. We are not supposed to grab for everything call it ours. I am sure you have heard about the many stories where being "I" has caused madness. We are not meant to be separated because in real life we are not. I am you as you are me. If we aren't supposed to be one and the same, our paths would never cross. We do not have to meet up physically to be connected. Everything connects to everything on its own.

We do not like it when we feel ill. Not even our most prized possession can offer the comfort we need when we are feeling under the weather. When we are sick, we do not feel physically connected to anything. In fact, this is when we often slip into rest—a place of nothingness with the self and with our thoughts. The feelings of illness take our minds off ourselves with the self. We start to long for the "we" feeling instead. We want to have company come visit. Having them come see us actually brightens our day.

I know a few people who have dedicated most of their lives to work. They work to earn lots of money. To them, time is money and life is money. However, as they get older and have all the money they worked so hard for—and that's it—they suddenly realize, then, that something is missing from their lives. Sure, they have financial security but who can they share it with? They suddenly wonder if working so hard for a cushioned bank account was really worth it.

By nature, we are meant to be social sharing people. However, when goods get bigger or more valuable (so we think), our sharing ways get greedy. Sharing may even stop altogether. We get nervous when we think precious goods will disappear. We want to hold onto them with tighter hands. Even if our neighbors are desperate, we selfishly hesitate before parting ways with our materialistic goods. When was the last time you shared something with someone? Did you offer up a lot of something or just a little because you didn't want it to all go away?

A few years ago, I took my kids to a James Bond-themed fireworks display at Harrods in London. At one point in the evening, we decided to get some beverages. With our drinks in our hands, we walk past a young homeless man who was sitting on the ground with his dog. Not once did he beg for money; he just sat there in his own little world, watching everyone pass by. He definitely caught my eye. I stopped in my tracks and asked one of my children to go and give him a few coins. My child was too shy to do it. I crouched down and guided my child's hand so that we placed the money in the man's lap. "Thank you," he said with a smile. I turned to my children and grinned. "What lovely manners he has," I said. I had always told my children that we are nothing without manners.

The fireworks were amazing. As we headed back to the train station, we happened to walk by the young man again. "Thank you and goodnight," I heard him say. I was blown away by the fact that he recognized us from the huge crowds, especially since we hadn't given him much money. His manners touched my heart and soul. I squatted down and wanted to get to know him better. I said hello, introduced myself, and asked him if there was anything he needed; the nights were getting colder. He thought a moment and then replied that he needed blankets and socks. I nodded and scribbled my phone number on a piece of paper. I told him that we would meet him at the same spot the following week with items that he needed. He thanked me a third time.

That week we rushed around, asking friends for any clothes or jackets they no longer wanted. We also bought a gas stove and some food. Furthermore, we proceeded to ask various charities if they had anything they could donate to the young man. We were able to get a dog leash, dog food, and even a can opener—many great essentials. Lastly, we went to the church hall and asked for donations. I was surprised by the frosty response I received.

"They don't *want* help," the churchwoman replied briskly. "I have worked in the soup kitchens!"

"It is not about changing how they choose to live. I would never tell you how to live your life," I explained. "It is about offering support and love no matter how we live. Humanity still lives." I think I got my message through to her. The vicar did give us a little bit of money, but that wasn't what we were after, anyway. We were looking for basic necessities.

The following Saturday, we eagerly took the train to meet up with the young man again. His name was Kevin. But suddenly we became a little anxious as we stood on the pavement, waiting for him to show up. What if he didn't? He did. We greeted him enthusiastically. He was so surprised that we kept our word. We chatted and he told us about his experiences and why he has chosen to stay living on the streets. He said that they offered freedom from the chains of life. We kept in touch for a good few weeks. Every now and then, he would call us to let us know what he needed. My children didn't quite understand why we were going out of our way to help him. I reminded them where I had come from; that could have easily been me sitting there on the streets. I would want to be treated with the same respect and manners as he had shown toward us that firework night.

We arranged to meet another time in the darkness of the night. I didn't want to be ignorant and asked him if he would be kind enough to show us where he lives. We went to a McDonald's restaurant first and got him a burger and fries. We also bought a burger for his dog. After we ate, we grabbed some hot drinks and began to follow him to his house. After a few turns down side roads, we finally arrived. A side doorway of a shop was his front door. He pulled out a few flat cardboard boxes for us to sit on, and we chatted and drank our beverages for some time. I felt very special as we sat inside his home and very humbled that he had allowed strangers to visit. He told us that he wanted to get his own place and that he wanted to find a job. Of course, we wanted to help him. I had the biggest smile on my face as we left to go home. This young man had no fear of materialism—no fear of anything, really. In that moment, we were just regular people, seeing each other as equals and enjoying hot cups of coffee.

While I knew about foster care systems and being an orphan quite well, I never really knew much about being homeless in a literal sense. I didn't know what kinds of systems were (or weren't) put into place to help these folks. I happened to jump into the deep end very blind. I wasn't exactly sure how I could help Kevin, I just knew that I wanted to. I looked in the phone book and found many numbers. I made dozens of calls and spoke to a bunch of helpful people along the way. I even wrote to the late Anita Roddick who owned The Body Shop. A businesswoman, human rights activist, and environmental campaigner, she had just done a documentary about the homeless and spent a week sleeping on the streets. I thought she would be more than happy to help this young man. However, the letter I received back from her secretary proved otherwise. She didn't want to know about him.

Finally, the homeless systems found Kevin and assured me they would help me. However, soon they were asking me for phone numbers they did not have. Different departments deal with different things. There are so many people working on so many different levels, and this is where breaks in the chain form. This is why people fall through the cracks. I didn't want to give up hope. I called various magazines to write an article about him and his situation. They would offer him enough money to get started. He called me up at the end of the week and I told him we would meet up with him again. This time, however, we would be bringing some good news.

We showed up at our usual meeting place and waited. Kevin never came. I was confused; this wasn't like him at all. We went to every McDonald's restaurant in the area and asked if he had been seen. I left notes in places I knew he frequented with hopes that he would get in touch with us again. We traveled to all the train stations we knew he sometimes spent time at. We finally stopped at a cluster of newsstands. We told the attendants about Kevin, how we had met him, and how we had been bringing him essentials from time to time. When we were done explaining who he was and why we were looking for him, one of the attendants said that he most likely had been removed from the streets by the police.

I left upset because this young man would now never know that we had tried our best to meet up with him again. I hope he got from our paths crossing as much as we got from meeting him. The experience showed me that humanity and manners are not dead no matter what side of the fence we're on. Kevin touched my heart and I thank him for welcoming us into his home. When he invited us over, we saw a home—not cardboard boxes. In fact, we saw a man with his dog in their castle. Those few weeks showed that it can be any of us. Security is in the heart, not the goods of the mind.

Respect should be given to everyone regardless of how they choose to live and no matter how different they may seem. Acceptance is the key. Remember, we are all the same. Humanity is about acceptance and respecting life. We all go the same as we came. The piece in the middle is the only thing that differs—the life experiences we choose to participate in before the next life.

Working alongside the systems of the homeless in the box of my home because I really wanted to help someone from my heart gave me a great sense of freedom. I had no rules; it was just me. I realized that where the free will is willing, it can move mountains. I will forever be grateful for meeting Kevin. Our worlds happened to meet in the middle below a moonlit sky. Meanwhile, everyone else walked past us, simply getting on with their lives.

Even in the darkness, everyone is noticed and accounted for. No one is ever truly alone or left out. We are all-important and have an important gift and story to share about life. Sharing costs nothing. We all have plenty. Sharing is fun and makes us equal. It isn't measured by money. Gifts that are shared tend to come from the heart. No matter how limited we are at seeing what is in front of us, our internal beacons of light guide us where to go.

Admittedly, I am directionally challenged. I tend to get lost often, and it doesn't matter whether I'm traveling by car or by foot. I had to drive on the A406, better known as the road I had successfully managed to avoid—up until that day. A friend needed to be picked up because her car had broken down. Terrified, I got in the car with my handwritten directions and began the anxiety-inducing trek. My fear grew by the minute and my legs shook with fright. I didn't even want to think about what I would do if I couldn't find my stranded friend!

As I drove past various roads and signposts, not recognizing any of them, my eyes in the light of day were in total darkness. I felt like crying; I was completely out of my comfort zone. All the drivers in the vehicles around me knew where they were going and what lanes to be in for their exits. I was blind. Suddenly, a little white feather landed on my windshield and tucked itself in one of my wiper blades. I smiled for the first time since getting into the car; the feather made me feel calmer and not so alone. During stressful times like that, I always associate random signs and gifts from my guide, Ramini. Even in the wind, that feather stayed with me during the drive, all the way until I saw my friend waving franticly at me. Utter relief washed over my body. And then, as gently as it had appeared, the feather blew away.

Even in daylight, I had been driving as if I were blind because the fear in me took over. Fear can leave us crippled and unsure of ourselves. That feather helped me along my journey to help my friend. It gave me strength when I needed it most. In hindsight, I just needed to believe in myself. We always come out of experiences stronger than when they began. We should embrace the many shades of light as we participate in our daily experiences. For fun, we should try and find what is called "pitch black"—the darkness everyone talks about. But we never will. This shade is just a shadow cast by the light.

∞

TWENTY-SEVEN

DEF-(DEATH)-AMATION OF CHARACTER

In my teenage years, I had many labels from the mouths of others. I wore them like clothes on my back—invisible clothes put on me against my will. No matter how much I tried to shrug these names off, they would just wrap around me tighter like a long snake, trailing behind and trying to make me trip up. I felt like I was being haunted, but not by ghosts; at least ghosts can be seen. Labels are invisible to the physical eye. However, they have the ability to make us feel trapped and confused, like being buried alive by words that don't belong to us.

Labels are words used by people who do not understand us very well. They are poisons of the mouth. If only the saying, "Sticks and stones will break my bones but names will never hurt me," were true. Instead, name-calling and bullying can be much more damaging to the mind than we realize. Labels can be more piercing than physical pain. With physical pain, at least the body heals after a scrape or fall. The mind, however, is so much more powerful than the limbs we use. The mind is connected straight to the heart. That is why labels feel so personal when we hear them. This is also why we begin believing them if they are repeated over and over again.

The words that hurt us deeply are usually the words we do not believe. We don't like not being seen or understood for who we know we really are. For example, when I was in elementary school, my best friend kept getting picked on by our English teacher. For some reason, the teacher was treating him unfairly in front of the whole class. I could tell the teasing was getting to my friend. And one day, my own patience had run out after the teacher was continuously picking on my friend.

That's it! I thought to myself. *I can't watch this one more time and do nothing about it.* I stood up from my chair, marched over to the teacher who was sitting at her desk at the front of the class, and kept my focus on what I wanted to do. The teacher locked eyes with me, waiting. "Leave my friend alone, you bully!" I warned her, loud enough for the whole class to hear. With that, I calmly turned around and sat back down in my seat. The class suddenly grew quiet; they were all in disbelief by what I had just done. The teacher said nothing, her mouth agape. A few seconds went by and then she immediately ordered all of us to get back to work. My friend and I smiled at each other. My point had been made.

This example shows that we all have the power to point out the truth—even to people who are in positions of higher power. They should know better. We need to look out for each other instead of sitting back and watching unacceptable behavior. Remember, we have a choice to use our voices for good. Our voices can create positive change. We must all stand up for our basic human rights and expect to be treated fairly in return.

Our character, or overall disposition, is unique to us. We create it, change it, work on it, and own it. People will respect us based on our character. Most of us hope that we are looked upon as individuals with good character; it means we are thought of as good people. Those who have bad character are generally not trusted. Others tend to not want to be around them, either.

DIVIDED, SEPARATED, SPLIT UP, SECTIONED

In middle school, I was ridiculed for being different from everyone else. Still, I showed up for school every morning. My friends and I all did our best to fit in but we were poor and labeled lower class. Furthermore, we had the reputation of being mischievous and messed about, always playing practical jokes and passing notes back and forth. We were constantly giggling and whispering whenever our teachers weren't looking.

One morning, it was Sports Day. We'd spend all day playing activities outside and competing in different events. This would be a chance for teachers to sit back and relax. We all quickly formed a line to see who would get picked for teams for the first game. Of course, the same faces and same names were called out first. The sporty students were always chosen first. None of us were considered sporty so we took our seats on the sidewalk curb. We sat there all day long, watching the popular kids have fun. Silently, we wished we would've been chosen to participate. There was one girl who was very athletic and pretty. She was one of the chosen ones. She also had a heart of gold. I envied her, wondering what it would be like to be in her shoes for just one day.

Many years later, we had our school reunion. A woman came through the doors in a wheelchair. I noticed that she was unable to do very much, yet she could still speak. She had multiple sclerosis.

I was familiar with it because my sister had the same condition. But what took me a minute to realize was that this woman used to be the girl I had been jealous of. Apparently, she got multiple sclerosis not long after graduation. Now she had such a different reflection from when we were in school. In fact, her entire life was different. But even though her life was different, I was able to easily see past the wheelchair because she was still the same as before. Her character remained fully intact. And that's what I had remembered most about her when we were in school.

It's crazy how life can suddenly change paths for us. These changes can take us by surprise when we aren't expecting them. Often these changes can help us come into our own. Other times, they are an extreme wake-up call for whatever reason. This takes me back to the day the whole world stood still on September 11, 2001. We were all glued to our TVs in disbelief. No, it was not a horror movie that we saw; it was real life in the United States. When two planes hit the World Trade Center, we watched live via streaming video as people stood on the outside ledges of the burning buildings, waiting to be rescued. We were haunted by visions of people losing their grips and falling to the ground. We heard the horrendous thuds of bodies landing on the pavement. I can't even imagine the sheer terror those people must have felt in their final moments. One minute they were at their office desks, the next they were clinging onto ledges, not knowing if they would see the next day.

What strikes me most about those terrible events is that I saw two people holding hands as they stood on a ledge. They were holding hands to comfort each other and to not feel so alone at that moment. They held each other's hand in love—a love of worth when faced with fear. It was just a simple act but it suddenly meant so much more than anything else. Their connection created a lifeline of love. This is the true meaning of "to have and to hold." It means to hold another person's hand within your own.

What is more important to us at the end of the day? The answer to this question usually suddenly becomes very clear in extreme circumstances. The words "If only . . ." come up when we are close to passing on. They come up when sudden changes occur. The divides occur by the rituals we now make our everyday lives. We can pick and choose what is most important to us based on what we feel inside our hearts. We have the opportunity to accept and express more love in our lives only if we choose to do so. We don't want to live with any regrets when it's time to cross to the other side of the fence, do we? Love is something we feel and don't buy. It is something unseen but always felt in feelings of the soul's heart. When we peel the layers away of our busy lives, there is only love.

Most things in life are divided and put into groups, standards, levels, labels, prices, abilities, ages, etc. A rule of life is to separate and divide us all up—to keep us apart even as we sleep. How apart our characters of life's meanings make us feel. Why do we turn to designer clothes to fit in? Why do we go out of our way and out of our comfort zones to belong or feel like we are a part of certain groups? We try to feel connected to life outside while then feeling disconnected to our lives on the inside. We think we need to get dressed up before we go out with friends who, ironically, all feel the same way. We drink to numb certain feelings, to hide the pain of love that isn't returned or understood. Sometimes, what is supposed to be a fun night out may turn into an evening of tears. All we want is to not be judged. We want to be understood for who we are. Most importantly, we want to be loved.

Michael Jackson sang words like this in the song, "Childhood." It was a song that resonated with me—a song that had great meaning to me—because it reminded me of my own childhood. I'm sure Michael felt similar; his childhood was taken away when he got into music and his career launched off. He was a man who was so misunderstood, that is, unless you had a lost childhood like he did. The child in him just wanted to play as any child would want to do. Adults who saw him as an adult did not understand him. Soon, everything was about money, not innocent childhood thoughts as Michael wanted.

Michael was loved for what he could give. Now that he's on the other side of the fence, he can now play like a little boy in peace; he is out of his adult physical body. Deep down, we all still have a little child in us who wants to play. Innocent children do not think the way we do, and we have to remember that. But sometimes a child's mind will get trapped inside an adult's body, like what happened with Michael, and then we label that person as different because it is not what we are used to. Their behavior is not what we call "normal."

Again, age is something that divides us up. We don't usually see many adults skipping down the street. They are afraid of being labeled as mad or freaks if they do so. So what though? Be brave and have lots of fun! Just because we are adults doesn't mean we suddenly have to live in doom and gloom. Fun is for people of *all* ages. We should explore the world in which we live and enjoy it to the fullest. We do not need to tell the children within us all to get lost when we grow up. In fact, we should embrace them.

Some of us suffer from tunnel vision of adults. We think that as we get older, we need to "grow up" and be serious all the time. The opposite is true. We should never take life too seriously! We have an essence and our unique character and we all love to laugh, even if we do try to stifle our giggles from time to time. Who says we have to stop smiling? The next time you're walking down the sidewalk, break into a skip for a few yards. I bet you'll start laughing and even make others laugh. And that will cause a positive chain reaction of good feelings.

Expectations come with a price. Love is life and life is love. Start by smiling for no reason at all. If you need a reason to enjoy yourself, smile for a smile's sake. If people look at you with funny faces, smile again. They'll be curious. *Why is that person smiling? What is so funny?* We all look much better and healthier when we smile instead of frowning. Remember back to when we played as children and were allowed to laugh. In fact, we were *encouraged* to laugh. Relish in those moments all over again.

If you are questioning your own character, think about your loved ones. Think about the words, *loved ones*. Clearly, if they love you, you are doing something right! You must have good character. Your friends and relatives loved you, too. And they still do, even on the other side of the fence. They would never want to harm or haunt you. Smile as you remember them.

Respect should be handed back to our loved ones in the afterlife. There are far too many labels that are hung around their bones. These labels do not reflect who they are. They just want to be heard like us. They may have crossed over but they still have voices. They want to tell us "I'm sorry," "I love you," or "I still look out for you." If we all knew the truth behind ghosts, we would start boiling water in our tea kettles and sit in our living rooms to chat and hang out with our afterlife friends and family members. To be fearful of ghosts is silly make believe. They are around to help and guide us in our physical lives.

We are all special, very important, and precious from the inside out. Labels come and go just like trends. We stand in our own footprints amongst many others. The difference is that our own footprints help define us and build our character as we continue our life experiences. I have a footprint that leaves its mark wherever I go and so do you. Together, we create paths that may divide us as we wake up each day. But when all is said and done on earth, our footprints will be side by side.

∞

TWENTY-EIGHT

IMAGINE

I thought I would talk about our imagination and visualization because we have two bodies—our physical bodies that we see as solid every day and our afterlife bodies, or the real us (more solid than our physical bodies). Remember, the afterlife body is often felt or sensed, yet it is not seen with the physical eyes. This raises the question, *But how do I use my afterlife body in sync with my physical body?* It's a logical question. After all, how can we use something our eyes can't physically see?

To answer this, I am going to take us back to when we were children. Do you remember being in a boring lesson at school? For me, Wednesdays were the worst. I had double science classes, followed by double chemistry ones—a subject I did not find easy! Oftentimes, I would find myself daydreaming about random things. I would stare out of the classroom window and just let my thoughts wander. In fact, many thoughts passed through my mind during this time, and they would often accompany picture thoughts, too.

I would visualize numbers as if written on a chalkboard in my mind. Looking at the numbers, I would then add up the sums. (Okay, I admit that I sometimes used my fingers for some of the addition.) Are you aware of how much thought process goes through our minds in a single day? Thoughts are going on in and around us *all* the time. In fact, we can become so consumed by them that we don't realize how much time actually flies by.

We may think we live in a world that is regulated by time. This is associated with the physical clock and various cycles that we have become accustomed to. However, in truth, our real bodies (our afterlife bodies) do not live in time as we know it. Time does not exist; only our *perception* of it does.

There have been times, like when waiting for the oven timer to sound, for example, that one minute can seem like ages. Or if we have to speak in public, three minutes can feel like three days. Sometimes, a day feels like it's gone in the blink of an eye. Time becomes flexible in the sense that our perception of time can change depending on what activities we are doing and how we feel about them.

During readings with people, I have noticed that we have talked for three hours—even though it only *felt* like one hour. Again, time is reflected by the experiences that we have and how we relate time to them. Earlier, we discussed frequencies and vibrations; I compared them to finding a specific radio station. To briefly touch on this again, say the physical vibration we use to experience our life experiences is an earth frequency; however, the afterlife body frequency is a different "station," so to speak. One is a slower frequency than the other. This raises the question: If our real afterlife bodies are of a higher frequency, meaning they are faster than our physical bodies, how are both of them ever meant to connect up?

Why do we function in the physical slower one? Well, it is the one that closely matches the earth's frequency. No wonder, then, why we separate the two bodies apart. We are told to meditate to find the key, or the portal, that connects us to our whole selves—connecting and balancing the physical body with the afterlife body. We are told to sit quietly, listen to relaxing music, or participate in meditative journeys to help us find the doorways to our real selves. However, if our minds don't understand this—all of the acting and visualization in the world—the concepts will still be difficult to grasp. We like to know how something works *before* we attempt to use it. This is why we have so many instruction manuals for the things that we buy.

Visualizing things in the mind, when practiced, is a tool to help us see what we see in thought rather than rely on what the eyes see for us. It is the mind that really sees in the physical world, anyway, not the eyes like we think. The eyes receive images that are then sent as messages back to the brain. Only after the brain has decoded these images do we see. If it were true that our eyeballs see for their own sake, why is it that my eyeballs need glasses? It is because the messages sent to the brain do not recognize the images. The seeing process is in the brain and not the eyes, after all. Make sense?

Our brains hold our actual sight, which is why the eyeballs are so closely connected to the brain in the first place. Electronic messages are sent to the brain very quickly; we believe and think our eyes really see. But all of the connections are actually happening *behind* the eye. Try this out just for fun. Stare at a random picture for five minutes, then close your eyes. I bet you still can see the image in your thoughts, right? But your eyes are closed!

The brain sees the world by what it remembers. Have you ever been asked by someone to look up in the sky at a plane, or a bird, or a rainbow and although that person is pointing at it for you to look at, no matter how much you look about your eyes can't see what that person sees? This is because the brain does not yet recognize or see what has been asked of it.

This brings me back to imagination. I am sure if you are anything like me you have at some point been scolded for daydreaming a time or two. Some people believe that dreams are for when we are asleep at night, not during the day. Okay, so why is daydreaming not called "night dreaming" then? Maybe it's because nights are days in other parts of the world. Furthermore, we usually rest the body while we dream. If that's the case, perhaps we should daydream more often! Time, in general, is always in the now regardless of if it's light or dark out. But because we are busy with our timetables and jam-packed schedules, we regard our experiences of activity as movement, even if we aren't fully aware of them.

We start any given day with getting dressed (yes, an activity in the now). Then we have breakfast (yes, an activity in the now). Then we go about our days (yes, an activity in the now). Then we have lunch (yes, an activity in the now). Then we get on with more schedules and tasks (yes, an activity in the now). Then we arrive home after our busy days (yes, an activity in the now). Then we have dinner (yes, an activity in the now). Then we may draw a bath (yes, an activity in the now). Then we relax and watch TV (yes, an activity in the now). Then we go to bed (yes, an activity in the now). It is at this point that we use our afterlife bodies more than our physical bodies to dream or use astral travel to visit with and talk to people who have continued life in the afterlife. Our real afterlife bodies do not need to sleep (yes, an activity in the now). In fact, our real bodies are alive and wide awake every day . . . all the time . . . *in the now*.

Have you ever gone to sleep only to wake up feeling like even though your physical body had rested, you feel like *you* stayed awake the whole time? At that moment, you probably just shrugged off the peculiar feeling and called it strange! But now I would like to get your mind's attention. Have you noticed when a physical body is pronounced brain dead? This means the physical body does not work or connect to its earthly body anymore. Some people are pronounced dead this way. However, this does not happen for the eyes if someone is blind. They are still connected even though there is a disconnect between the eyes and the brain. Blind people can still go about their days just fine.

Basically, the brain in the physical sense is where it is all going on. The brain sends messages throughout the whole body, telling it how to function. But how much thought do we *really* give our marvelous brains? When we get headaches, we take painkillers to feel better. Do we take them to numb nerve endings, perhaps?

Now it's time for a little imagination and visualization exercise. I want to show you how to connect with the whole of you—your physical side and your afterlife side at the same time. When we utilize our whole bodies, we are able to have access to more of us and that of life. Remember that our minds, our thoughts, our imagination, and our visualization equals our creation.

Would you be surprised to know that we tend to go through our earthly experiences not using or accessing our afterlife bodies very much? We see the physical body like we see the earthly world, as physical, and we assume that anything we can't see, feel, touch, or hold must not be real—or so we think. If no one can physically see what we see in our thoughts, we tend to not talk about them. Why? It's because we don't have actual evidence to show people; and therefore, our thoughts have a difficult time getting validated by others. We also don't want to come across as weird.

I want to encourage you to be aware of your thoughts because your thoughts connect you to your real wholeness. Your thoughts may come across as visual pictures and images. Even if they only flash in your mind every now and then, these thoughts are the gateway to your wholeness that connects your physical body to your afterlife body. Embrace them and try to understand them. They will only benefit you.

Compare us to a seed that is planted in the physical world. It is watered and nurtured and grows into a physical body (a human baby), which then grows and grows even more. Try to imagine a twister funnel that starts off as a point at the base, similar to our seed. As the funnel fans out, it resembles us as we grow. We collect information and become part of life's experiences. Here, we also collect other people's thoughts and expectations of us and of the world. If we spin this funnel from the base very fast, the wide span will spin faster out like a whirlwind collecting everything in its path. This is a metaphor to explain why we find it hard to understand how to connect to another frequency of our afterlife being.

If you can imagine looking at the base of the funnel as the physical us, moving at a slow frequency pace (meaning slower than the afterlife frequency), then the wide part consists of all the earthly activities and experiences that we have. Depending how active we are, we may be busy in thought all the time (mental hyperactivity) or we may be hypo-physical (never stopping or slowing down) so the top part of the funnel is moving way faster than the physical vibration of us. The base of the funnel—our physical bodies—are moving on a frequency of, for example, 95.8. The rest of the funnel—the experiences of us—is moving faster than the physical base, for example, at 99.00 At the top above the funnel, and around it, are our afterlife bodies. They are moving at 100.00, faster than the physical base and the rest of the funnel. We can now see and understand how the frequencies work at their attunement.

This is the same for us because, deep down, we remember that our physical bodies have a slower frequency than our real afterlife bodies. We try to compensate for this by keeping busy, by speeding up what we are doing, and taking on more and more. We end up having very little time or space for anything else other than what we have committed ourselves to doing. Sometimes, we suddenly feel like our brains are on autopilot and won't switch off. This is all about the flow of the frequency we are on. If someone says to us, "Hey, go and meditate by doing this . . ." we wonder why and how?

When we are on our own, why we find this hard to do? If we are taught the difference between the frequencies, maybe we would understand how to connect to this other frequency a bit more. Subconsciously, we always feel like we have to keep doing . . . searching . . . and finding out information. Remember, we hold the volumes of life of all of our experiences in our own internal libraries. These volumes wait patiently for us to remember and open up your minds to take a look.

As with anything, this takes practice. Just like when we tune in to a radio station, we have to be patient and listen carefully to the frequency until what we hear makes sense and sounds like the station we are looking for. Receiving messages is a lot like listening and waiting for symbols, images, pictures, or messages in thought. Mediums do a lot of pausing . . . waiting . . . and listening when communicating with the afterlife people. It's quite the opposite of what we do in our everyday lives that are so focused on go, go, go!

To reach the real us—to connect to the real and the whole of us—is about slowing down rather than speeding up. It is about slowing and calming our thoughts so that we can see a lot more than in the whirlwind crowdedness of our thoughts. These thoughts can be our own or mixed with thoughts from everyone we communicate with.

Really, it's about knowing and being aware of and recognizing our own frequencies that are personal to us. Our direct line extensions, so to speak, run through the base of our physical bodies and up through the physical earthly experiences of matter right to the top of us and into the open space of all life. Perhaps this is what the symbols of the chakras mean? Our cores, or our centeredness, help us how to remember and connect to all that we are. Do the eyes see, after all? Are our minds our most precious gifts? It's about understanding how everything works internally and externally. We try to make frequencies work for us rather than against us. Whatever frequencies we choose become a part of who we are.

Finding the balance and attunement between the various frequencies is a journey traveled in the mind. Using our imaginations, we have the ability to travel to any place we want to go. Just because we may not be able to see something as physical matter does not mean that we are mad. Our imaginations give us freedom. If you have ever questioned something as real or being a part of your imagination, it shows you have gotten hold of your own tuner. With a little bit more practice, you will then recognize it is not your imagination. It is the attunement process. At first, it only feels like it's the imagination because we are entering the mind rather than the physical of matter that we are more used to.

We should Enjoy our daydreams and our imaginations for as long as we can. These keys are used to unlock and reconnect us to the attunement of the whole of us. They help make our physical/afterlife connections more direct. They even help remove all the clutter and reconnect us to our cores. Remember, our cores run through the base of the physical body and all physical matter, ultimately connecting to the afterlife body of who we *really* are.

Sweet dreams are made of direct connections between the physical body and the afterlife body. Our creations start from seeds of thought. Our imaginations hold the keys to unlock our brains' potential. These keys have the ability to open up even more of us should we choose to explore ourselves deeper. We have the power to experience anything we want to experience, so what are we waiting for?.

∞

TWENTY-NINE

How to Silence the Mind

We have gone on a long and winding journey so far, exploring the many layers we have with our minds, thoughts, feelings, expressions, body language, and the language we use to express all of these. This next journey is about how we access our own personal doors, or portals. It is about using both of our bodies at the same time. We will explore more of ourselves past the walls of the physical body and mind, breaking through the barriers of the physical materialistic matter.

We can have access to whatever is inside of us, to see and experience so much more while participating in the experiences of our earthly journeys. With time, we remember more of who and what we are. We may often hear how to do certain things by listening to CDs or reading books, yet we still often find our minds wandering off. We daydream in our own worlds of thought of the physical everyday mind issues. Yes, we may feel relaxed, but that doesn't mean we are *connected*.

So, what's missing? Imagine we have a computer and we want to download some photos onto it from our digital camera. We usually need a connection—a cord that plugs into the USB connection to the computer—so that the information flows and travels into the computer memory via the cord. When we listen to self-help techniques on CD, we are not given the cord so that we can properly "download" information into our brains. We have a missing link and connection. This enables the mind to do two things at once: listen to the CD and wander off in our own thoughts of our daily lives. We now have two separate things going on at once.

To download and access information properly, we need to be able to shut down other programs going on in our minds before we even start to download and access our own self-portals, or doorways to our true selves. We're familiar with the saying, "One door closes and another one opens," right? Well, this is true. The same goes for our thoughts and how we access new programs that we don't understand yet. If we don't slow down and focus on one thing at a time, we run the risk of having too much going on, and this is where crossed wires can come in.

Here are the steps to access our self-remembering connections to our true selves:

1. Find a peaceful place away from distractions. It may be in a quiet field out in the open or on your bed before going to sleep. (Remember to turn off your cell phone and anything else that could potentially disturb you.)
2. Lie on the bed or sit in a comfortable chair—whatever is the most relaxing for you. Wear loose, comfortable clothes so that your body does not feel restricted.
3. Dim the lights or turn them off completely—whatever is comfortable for you. You want to make the room a relaxing

environment where you feel calm, safe, and at ease with your own personal space and atmosphere.

4. When you feel connected to your room—meaning settled and completely comfortable—slip off your shoes and lie down on the bed (or sit on a chair where your body is fully supported). If you're anything like me, I find it really hard to *totally* relax my physical body. Don't worry; we are concentrating on the mind first. Listen to your body and embrace what works for you.
5. Once you have settled yourself down comfortably, don't worry if you fidget a lot at first—this is normal. The body is just adjusting to slowing down from a busy day.
6. Take as long as you like. There is no rush . . . no panic . . . no timeframe. Relaxing takes practice. In fact, practice is the body's way of remembering.
7. Be aware how your body feels while you are resting in your comfortable position. How do your limbs feel? Is your heart rate slowing down? How much are you moving? What is going through your mind? Try to clear everything out of your mind. Just observe what your body is doing naturally rather than fight it. Try to let go of resistance.
8. This is the important part. Try to move your focus off your movements and begin to focus on your heartbeat. How does it feel? Can you hear it?
9. Move on to your breathing. Concentrate on the sound of it. You should be relaxed enough to be able to travel with me on a journey of you. Can you remember a time when you were ever floating out on the sea? If not, imagine what it would be like. Think of its rhythm . . . its flow . . . its movement. Compare it to your breath. Do they seem similar? Focus on the ebb and flow of life's source and energy.

10. As you breathe . . . in . . . and . . . out . . . in . . . and . . . out . . . be aware of your own rhythm and flow. Feel it. Concentrate and focus purely on this function, trying to ignore the rest of your bodily movements. Consume your mind's thoughts into the flow of your breathing as if you have shrunk and entered into your breathing. This is your energy field and life force connection of you. Don't worry if this does not happen straight away; try this exercise for as long as you enjoy it. This may be for five minutes or anything up to an hour. If you drift off to sleep, so be it. There are no rules! Let your body guide you as to when you have had enough.
11. Once you have managed to connect to the flow of your body—when your mind is stilled enough from physical thought and only focused on the thoughts of your breathing—let your main attention be on your breathing while your physical thoughts run in the background. This is where practice comes in.

The more you practice this form of meditation, the more your physical thoughts will be silenced. When you inhale, it will feel like waves rising up, lifting your entire body. When you exhale, it will feel like waves moving out. The rhythmic waves of your own breathing, when practiced, will feel like you're on waves. Once you have reached this level, you will have slowed your body down to match your inner frequency and balance. The connection of all of your senses of your afterlife body will then make the connection with your physical body, thus allowing you to travel freely *within* rather than out.

Note that it is important *before* you access the inside of you to have an idea of what you want to explore. This connection opens up the universal web of you, similar to when we access the Internet. We can open up *anything*. If there are parts of you that have been hidden for any reason, these things can surface when you access your universal internal web. In fact, this happened to me many years ago.

I had always tried to keep the secrets of my childhood buried deep inside of me. Those memories were dark and painful; I didn't want anyone to know about this part of my life. I also didn't want to remember or face it all over again. I wanted to deny it had even happened to me. I divided and separated myself from the orphaned and abused child in me as if she didn't exist. I attempted to forget she was ever a part of me.

I believed I could run away from her if I distanced myself from those memories by creating new ones. I figured time would help her disappear. I was getting older every year, therefore a year more of distancing myself from my childhood and the experiences I had would make me forget. I didn't realize that she would *always* be connected to me no matter what I tried to do to deny it.

Deep down, I knew I would have to face that little girl and all of those repressed memories someday; I just didn't want that day to ever come. I kept putting it off because I knew it would be painful. Yet, because this experience had caused such a divide within myself, the only way to close it was to go back to the point where the divide occurred. I finally realized that once I faced my demons, I wouldn't have to run away from *me* anymore. In fact, I would be able to accept myself for who I was despite my flaws and dark past. But none of this was easy. It took me approximately ten years to face myself. It was a hard journey to go on alone, but I am grateful that I did it.

The first time I became aware of this journey of self-exploration was when I went to a spiritualist church. It had healing sessions going on. Well, everyone in the church was taking a turn; I knew I could not escape or run away like I had always done. Panicking, I felt trapped and pinned against the wall. I started to get agitated because I didn't want to actively participate like everyone else. I was scared of the healer and didn't want her to know about my past or and have access to all my secrets and experiences. I mean, I had worked *so* hard to keep my past hidden from everyone. And then it was my turn . . .

I sat on the chair as the healer put her hands on me. I shut my eyes in total fear. Suddenly, she told me to look at the little girl in me—the one who was four years old. As soon as she said this, for the first time ever, I saw *me*. I was a little blond girl who was full of innocence., standing by a tree. But instead of embracing the little girl I saw in my mind, I *hated* her. In fact, I wanted to kill her! I wanted to hurt her and beat her so hard that she would die. I was so shocked at my response and how much anger I felt toward the little girl in me that I instantly realized I still had a serious issue from my childhood: I hated myself.

These feelings all stemmed back from how people treated me. My reaction toward the vision of me as a child was also based on how others treated me. Pure hatred. Wanting me dead. I was worthless. My feelings were memories given to me by other people. These thoughts left me hating me . . . disowning me . . . and separating me from me. I didn't exist. The only people I saw who existed were the random people I met in my everyday experiences. I did not see me anymore. And although I didn't die physically, I died inside. My connection to me was severed and hung lifelessly by a thin thread. I had never expected to see myself as that little four-year-old girl. No, I was not expecting it at all. The experience jolted me.

My extreme reactions toward myself and my feelings of such deep hatred—the total opposite of how I like to be—really made me open my eyes. Suddenly, I found myself making excuses to the healer and everyone in the church as tears rolled down my cheeks. I was totally out of my depth and could not contain my own feelings anymore. I ran out of the church and drove straight home, unsure of how I was supposed to handle what had just been unleashed. What was I supposed to do with these emotions? How would I be able to bury these memories all over again? All of the negative experiences had unexpectedly resurfaced in me during that healing experience.

At home, I ran a bath. Every ounce of me was filled with hatred that I did not know how to cope with. I had never experienced this amount of hatred toward myself, especially not on this deep of a level before—to the point of wanting to kill me as a child. I had wanted to kill the girl I had briefly connected with that day. I cried so much, having no idea what to do with myself. I slipped into the hot bath and felt at a total loss and so emotionally unstable. This is what the experience of healing had brought out in me, a hatred that had been buried . . . denied . . . and now, for the first time, revisited and remembered. I had now visited a very dark place in me—a place that felt like hell. Only one thing was for certain: I didn't ever want to visit that place again. However, the tiny voice inside of me whispered, *One day you know you'll have to*.

If I wanted to heal the hatred toward myself and the little child inside of me, I had to let go of feelings toward myself that didn't belong to me personally—feelings that had been programmed into me by other people. I had to remember and believe that these feelings belonged to them, not me. In order to accept and release the past, I had to visit it all over again—that dark place of hell within myself. While it was a very hard journey, it was a very cleansing one after I was finally able to begin the healing process. Remember, the experience depends on the amount of healing needed and what experiences caused the trauma of separation of the self in the first place.

Before you embark on any form of healing or self-help connection through meditation, please think about your life experiences so far and if you have experienced any traumas that may be buried like mine. If you do, make sure you are not alone and that you have a safe support network of family members or friends who you trust enough to hold your hand as you journey into you and experience healing.

My experience nearly sent me over the edge. What was supposed to be an innocent healing session at a spiritual church could have done much more harm than good. Luckily, I didn't have any suicidal thoughts or depression. However, I definitely did lose my mind. But, in the end, I was strong enough to work through it—even though there was *a lot* to sort and clear out.

Please be aware of yourself and how healing works. It is not something to be scared of, but responsibility, care, and aftercare are needed before, during, and after the healing process. I strongly feel that any form of healing needs a backup system of aftercare even if it is just reading a brochure of how a healing treatment can make you react and feel. I am glad things turned out the way they did for me. My experience opened up a healing door I never thought I would be able to open. But I must say this again: Healing has a responsibility to offer a support backup plan for people in case they experience a reaction like I did.

The mind has the ability to clear any blockages inside of the self. When people talk about energy blocks within the chakras, or the body, they are usually talking about emotional or trauma experience blocks that are buried deep inside. These blocks keep us from our true whole selves. They also keep us from reaching our full potential by creating barriers in the forms of negativity, depression, and self-harm. These barriers are often caused by a past experience, one that has been forgotten or intentionally buried. If not dealt with, they eventually form divides inside of us, divides between the physical body's life experiences that are felt with feelings and the connection of the universe, or our real afterlife bodies.

To connect the two bodies together is a process of stilling the mind by slowing it down. The movies of our lives are known to the present day enough so that they do not harm us in our everyday experiences. We deal with past blocks in different ways. However, it is comforting to know that the whole body has the ability to reconnect back to the whole self so it can remember and explore what it knows already.

Put simply, imagine that you are on an empty road. You walk up and down this road freely and regularly. But one day, someone randomly puts a big rock in the middle of the road. You didn't see the rock get placed there and, not being aware of it, you trip over it and fall hard on the ground. At first, you feel stunned and then confused. And then you look at your wounds. All of this happened because *someone else* put a rock on *your* road. The entire experience begins to create many thoughts, feelings, and reactions inside of you. You may begin to put additional rocks on your road to mirror what happened, and soon it becomes a bit like a dumping ground. However, after some time passes, you look at your road and it's not how you remember it being years ago. That memory has gone. Your new memory only sees and remembers this road with many rocks, or blockages, in its path—a road that you could once walk freely but not anymore.

This rocks-in-the-road metaphor is a lot like how our minds operate. Our minds are our own personal roads that we walk down every day. These roads start off smooth, clear, and easy to walk up and down. However, as we experience more in our physical lives, the roads of our minds can often get potholes, cracks, and eroded sections with every thought, word, and action that gets stored inside.

Think back to the breathing exercise mentioned above. Remember, we are like an ocean with our individual currents that run deep to the depths of the ocean floor. On the surface of the water, we do not notice what is underneath; we are too busy bobbing around. But when we dive down underneath the surface, we are able to see a whole different world. We forget so much of what we have because we tend to live and function primarily on the surface. Only our feet splash around in the deeper parts of our personal seas.

If you are going to go deep sea diving inside the sea that makes up you, be prepared. Make sure you have your life jacket, or your support system of family and friends. The journey under the sea is an amazing one that is full of life—the whole of the universe. Only when we face and accept ourselves for who we truly are will we be able to explore life in all its eternity. The biggest secret to self-freedom is to not be scared of ourselves. Ironically, this is where fear hides. Freeing ourselves frees us from fear itself. It's that simple. Enjoy your personal journey. It's a film never to be forgotten.

∞

THIRTY

The Afterlife Body Feels What the Physical Body Does Not See

We all know we feed our physical bodies with food for energy, filling our bodies up like fuel so we are able to experience many things each day. We know that certain foods can make our bodies react in different ways. Some give us a boost while heavy meals, for example, have the ability to make us feel sleepy. Other foods sustain us for hours while there are some that make our bodies feel hollow; we end up grazing all day. Whatever we consume, we will always *feel* some kind of a reaction.

This takes me to food and our afterlife bodies. Do you know how we nourish our afterlife bodies? I can tell you it's not with food! It is with *feelings* of experience within our many layers of situations and circumstance. These feelings are within the many facets, frequencies, and vibrations that give us meaning to our lives. Think of it as a film we create with sequences. Combined, these sequences map out our lives. Each frame unfolds into the next frame of experience that we want to feel, depending on whether it is for the self or to aid another person with whom we share a sequence of life. These films are personal to us and have no end. Remember, life is a continuation in the afterlife.

The day we all are brave enough to face ourselves full on—not in shame, guilt, shyness, or any other form of negative feelings toward the self—is a day we will feel the true meaning of love. When we can look at our own pictures of true self-worth and see and, more importantly, *understand* who we are and why we are here, we will find our inner peace. When we see our true selves naked with all of their quirks and vulnerabilities, and when we see past our physical frames, a colorful vibration will appear. That light is a feeling of total love. It is a feeling like no other.

When we can accept and open up ourselves to feel love toward the things that we regard as not perfect, we can embrace life for what it is. When we understand that we are not our physical bodies, we can then understand that we are not our experiences. Experiences are a reflection of what we feel. And if we realize that we are not what we physically look like . . . and we are not our experiences . . . then we can understand that we are total consciousness. We are total feeling. We are total truth and knowing. We are total love. In fact, we are the total of everything that we have forgotten.

If we can grasp at least a small fraction of our total beingness, then we would understand why we do not need fear in our lives. We all know about our planet earth. We all know as much as we can about our solar system. This is all our physical eyes can see and make sense of. We have a loose understanding that our universe is huge based on what we know and are told by NASA. But what we *really* know is equivalent to the size of a postage stamp. We are, indeed, miniscule in the grand scheme of things.

Imagine the total of life and that the universe is a big housing block that holds many buildings. It is a complex structure built to hold the many facets of life. Here, everything is in sync, connected, and interlinked. Earth, as we know it, is one house, and all the other planets are flats. There is the power house of the sun; we also have the moon, which is space dumping ground. The moon collects the universe's waste and byproducts, including any element such as water, rock, mineral, or vegetation. It does not matter what the moon collects. It is simply a store house of what the universe does not need. This will grow in time as it collects more and more waste. It can be looked at as a reserve, or it can be looked at as a collection of waste. It looks bright in the sky because of what it reflects. At the same time, it looks dark without much life. We know that worms feed and digest to create life in our compost piles; the moon is no different than this. If a new building, or planet, needs materials, this can be taken from the moon's collection.

We regard our personal houses and the towns and cities in which we live as large. Our countries are even bigger. Of course, it is difficult to imagine just how enormous the earth and the entire solar system are. But the space *inside* of us is bigger than all of the earthly life we see. This space makes us who we are. It is the true life source of all total life. We only use what we feel we need. We only know or understand what we want to remember. This is why we can sometimes feel limited. It is because deep inside every one of us, we all know the truth that we are so much more than we lead ourselves to believe.

We know earth but there are other earths that have different experiences to us that live differently. Each house is a place to experience—to remember the wholeness of who we are. There are many houses of learning, many schools of the universe. They are all a part of the total of all life. Zooming back, so to speak, into our own personal houses on earth shows how small everything is. We are like ants to the greatness of all life.

I have seen on another planet how people live so differently from us. They do not have wired electricity. Instead, they use magnetic energy. In fact, the walls of their homes are magnetic with built-in celled memory banks. New gadgets are coded up to the main frame circuit. Magnetic homes make a simple way of life. Transportation is through magna lines. Everyone works the same hours; everyone has the same free time. In return, whatever people need is provided for in return for their skills. This is truly a community planet where everyone works together. However, the one downfall is that this planet is still controlled by dictators who hide behind power.

When the truth of life is felt inside—when we are able to remember who we are without having any fear to hold us back—nothing in the universe can harm us. Our afterlife bodies have many pages, or layers, to them. Even though one page may get torn out, or screwed up, these pages only represent experiences; they cannot destroy us. What holds the pages together is the body and casing of the book—our essence. This energy, or frequency of life, is something that we can always tap in to.

The more we zoom away from the physical, the more we see our wholeness. This brings me back to fear—fear of ourselves, others, the unknown. How are we meant to remember the whole of life if we are stuck in the glue of fear? Remember all the fearful experiences you have been afraid of. The experiences happened, left an imprint in your memory, and then you moved on. We are in the present, looking ahead to the future. However, in truth, we live in the past, present, and future simultaneously.

There have been times when I have found myself in certain situations where I have felt like I was being pulled in two directions—part of a tug-of-war within myself. In fact, I have chosen relationships, at times, from both side of the fence. The physical side of the fence may choose a relationship to help aid healing from a past physical experience. At the same time, the afterlife side of the fence may choose a relationship to help another person connect with their feelings and emotions. On the surface, this can cause conflict and a battle of the wills from all angles within the relationship.

The afterlife side wants to share love, thoughts, and feelings to reflect the other person's love seen inside his or her shell of the physical. This is what the afterlife body of the other person has asked for. However, the physical side of this person does not remember and only remembers loss or lacking. In the end, a reflection of love and comfort is alien to what they want to remember.

All we really need to remember, no matter what type of relationships we find ourselves in, is that they are perfect to help us to understand more about who we are. We need to remember when we look back on a past relationship how much more the experience opened us up and enlightened us. However, we don't always choose relationships on a physical level. We may *believe* we have done so, but our choices are governed by what our bodies—both physical and afterlife—need more of. For example, if the physical side needs healing of some kind, this side will be more dominant in our choice for a partner. We will look for a partner with healing qualities.

If the afterlife body needs to experience giving or more knowledge, then the people we attract to us will mirror our desires. Sometimes, the physical and afterlife bodies may want healing, for example, at the same time. In this case, we choose with *feeling*. We choose someone who needs feeling just as much as we want to give it. The physical actions received will not match the deep feelings offered. Subconsciously, we know this relationship will ultimately be a short film, but due to our needs, we will try to hold on to this relationship longer than we need to.

Life experiences are fed all the time with our thoughts and feelings. Because of this, physical effects have the power to touch nerves of fear and cause people to react in fear. Love can quickly lead to fear if we do not follow our hearts and listen to our inner voices. Fear is our nerve of life. The question is, do we have the nerve to face fear within and pull it out of our bodies? Remember, that fear is nothing; it has no power.

Furthermore, the universe a big powerhouse. We are all plugged in to life. All I am trying to do is encourage everyone to turn their electricity *on*. Don't be afraid to experience more and remember more of the truth of life. Whether we choose to flip our switches on or not does not matter. What is important is that we are plugged in for all eternity. Our cords to the universe—the universe with no time—have all the patience in the world for us to remember when we so desire with our free will and choice. We really do already have everything we need in life.

If we do not like something in life, we have our plugs. And there are many extension cords to plug in to, so to speak—extension cords with no ends. We can simply pull the plug on whatever we do not like, especially if it's something that does not benefit us. Remember, we have the power to create the lives we desire. We meet the universe of life halfway, and we are never alone as we go through our experiences. Life consists of many films that are played over and over again. These films are reflections of us, but they are not us as whole.

When we remember how safe we are, we have remembered what life truly is. We can explore the many houses and planets in the universal home of life. In true life, we do not need machines and cars or spaceships. All we need is the power of knowing that what we desire is what we can create and experience. This is why when people meditate they can travel around the world via astral travel all while sitting in the same spot. Through the power of our free will and choice, we can remember and unlock the doors to the many universal houses in order to visit whomever we want to communicate with.

Everyone remembers the truth in their own time. And whether we remember now or not, our eternal connections keep us safe. It is up to us to break the chains of our lives in order to explore more of life past our physical houses, streets, cities, countries, and beyond. We are total life hidden in the physical cloak we think we know as life. But now we have an idea of how powerful free will and choice are. The powerhouse of life is inside everyone and everything; it is cocooned in various frequencies that make up our personal uniqueness. While we may feel an experience that knocks us down, we always have the power to stand up again.

Some things we like, some we do not. Some things appear frightening, while others seem basic. But the reflections of life make up the films created by the experiences that we have. These films are unique; we should sit back and enjoy them. Life, in general, is to be enjoyed, not lived in fear of the mind as hell. The cinema of life is playing many films. We should try and remember the titles of what we see—horror, fantasy, funny, fiction. There are many titles to choose from through our free will and choice.

Choose well and enjoy the food of life!

∞

THIRTY-ONE

Cold Calling—Do You Know Me?

Knock, knock . . .

I hear a sudden knock on the door and get up to go answer it. Opening the door, I smile. "Hello. Do you want to speak to me?" I ask.

"Ah, yes! It's you I've come to see, madam," a man replies pleasantly.

I nod and open the door wider. "How do you do on this fine day?"

"Very well, thank you. Although, it is cold outside today, wouldn't you say?"

"Please, come inside!" I exclaim. "What is your name?"

"Oh, here is my card," the man says, fumbling into his pocket. "It explains all about what I do. This visit shouldn't take too long."

I squint at the man's picture on the card. "This picture does look like you," I grin. "Although I can see you better in the flesh rather than your image on this card!"

The man smiles. "It's an old picture," he says. "My gray hairs have surfaced so well!"

With a chuckle and a handshake, we sit down to chat.

"Would you like a cup of tea?" I quickly ask, remembering my manners.

"Yes, thank you," he says as he begins rearranging a bunch of papers on his lap.

"Milk and sugar? What would you like?"

"A splash of milk is just fine, thank you. No sugar for me. My doctor told me to cut back for my health. It's not so good these days, I'm afraid . . ." he explains.

"Aw, that's a shame," I say. I bring him over his cup of tea. "Here you go. Please, have a snack, too. I have a variety of different kinds of biscuits here." I point to a plate.

"Thank you so much!" he says. "You know, I will take one, if you don't mind?"

I smile and point to the plate again. "Now what would you like to speak with me about?"

"Oh, yes . . . This is a courtesy visit from our management team. We would like you to be one of our valued customers. In fact, we have a discounted plan to offer you! Your age is perfect to join up now. You see, a good health plan covers all the costs of your funeral when you die. It helps take the burden of extra expenses away from your family," he says, pausing to make sure I'm following him.

"Go on . . ." I urge.

He continues. "This plan is new and it has so many benefits. With such hard times, this is a plan to cover an eco-funeral; the cost is kept low. I'm sure that you want to make a contribution to the planet when you die, right? This plan is perfect for you. Here, here's a leaflet. Would you like to take a look? If you have any questions while you look and we sip our tea, please ask away! I will help answer any questions you may have."

I begin flipping through the leaflet that he hands to me. A smile creeps across my face. *Shall I play a game with him?* I think to myself. *Sure, why not?* Looking up, I embrace the stare of his expectant face.

He thinks I'm ready to sign up for the eco-funeral plan. He leans forward on the edge of his seat, waiting for my reply. He thinks this is a done deal; I can see it in his eyes. His handy dandy leaflet sells it all. Heck, there's not much work left for him to do except collect my signature and shake my hand one last time. Polite manners are all he needs to convince me to join this plan, to give my family financial security after I am done with my physical body.

"Well, sir," I say calmly. "This plan seems to suit half of me—my physical side. However, I'm afraid this policy is null and void; it only counts if I die. I can assure you, I won't ever die! I just won't need my physical body anymore. This leaflet explains all about death. It's inaccurate!"

A puzzled face stares at me. "What do you mean, madam?" he asks slowly. "Please do not worry; this is for you. I have your name and date of birth in front of me. This form is correct, I can assure you. You'll see, we have the perfect plan for you! You can have it at such a low cost. One lump sum is guaranteed to cover all of your funeral costs. Madam, we all will die someday, you know? This is true. That's why we have burials and funerals each day. It's a given fact that comes to us all!"

'Sir, yes, it does look like the form is right. Yes, that's my name and my date of birth is correct. Everything is accurate for the physical side of me; that much is true. But there are many more details and much more of me that you don't know about—more than this form or your eyes that do not see clearly . . ." I say. My voices trails off as I wait for his reaction.

The poor man is totally lost now. I continue, amused with myself. "Sir, you have been trying to speak with the half of me who tends to forget important things. Let me introduce you to my *real* solid half. This plan is good through the eyes of people who have forgotten, however, I remember all of me. This form would not work for the real me," I say. I pause and let my words sink in. "Yes, I agree that my physical body will be done with down the road. But the real me will continue life for all eternity. I won't be ashes and dust. I will be real and getting on with my day with my other body that you cannot see. Do you understand what I'm saying? This form should say not 'in death will it pay.' To be accurate, it should read, 'after the transition has been done and when my physical body has had enough.' My real half will set me free. I will then be able to continue my life as we all know it to be."

The man stares at me, trying to read me. "Please, madam. I will have to step in and speak to my management team about this. This does not make any sense to me. I mean, life is life. We all know 'in death,' as this form says. That is how it's always been . . ." he says. He seems anxious. Perhaps he's realizing he won't get his sale as easily as he thought he would.

I shake my head in disagreement and shrug. "Thank you, sir, for speaking to my physical half. Unfortunately, the afterlife half—the *real* me—wants to laugh at how false this plan is. I really cannot agree to these terms when I know I live eternally."

The man sighs and rolls his eyes. "Well, madam, I really have to go. I have other customers to see. Thank you for the biscuits and tea," he says rather curtly.

"You're welcome, sir, and thank you for the chat. Sorry you only wanted to talk to half of me. Please call again when your policy has changed from 'in death' to 'in the transition into another experience of life'!"

Mumbling under his breath, the salesman gets up to leave. He starts walking toward the door.

I grin and call out, “Sorry, sir! I didn’t catch what you just said? Anyway, sir, have a lovely day! One day, you will see the truth and remember and know me . . .”

∞

EPILOGUE

RIP

My dad used to call me a sleeping princess. His words have fallen silent in the air, but they are words I still hear inside of me. I will never forget them. In fact, I often sift through our memories and reach out to him when I'm feeling lost or miss him. I know he will always be there for me, watching over me, waiting.

Excitement fills my chest and a huge smile spreads across my face. I hold out my hand as I skip along the path on the grassland. My dad's hand reaches out for me. "Dad!" I call out. It has been a long time since we last saw each other. "Have you finished work for the day? Can we have some fun today?" I am so happy to see him that I feel myself glowing with love. We have a bond so strong that it's impenetrable, like steel.

"Yes! Dad is home, princess. I told you so!" he says.

Wow, my dad didn't forget after all. He kept his promise and found me. We play in the grass at the back of our house. I wear an oversized hat on top of my head, shielding me from the rays of sunlight all around us. My legs run with long, rhythmic strides. Suddenly, my dad catches me and lifts me off my feet.

"Hello, princess," he says with a grin, planting a big kiss on my cheek.

I wrap my arms around his neck, squeezing with all my might. My face looks deep into his eyes. "I love you this much all around you," I say, stretching my arms apart as far as they go. My dad's eyes are soft and twinkle with love. I see and feel a magic that fills every cell of me—an imprint logged in my memory bank forever. We share a love that I will always carry around with me wherever I go.

My bum rests on my dad's sturdy shoulder blades, and I feel on top of the world. My head peaks out from around his, allowing me to see the world so far and wide. I see rooftops; I see everything. I am bigger than the adults who pass us by. My dad walks with a purpose, his long legs make me feel like I am on a roller coaster ride! The air rushes around my face, pushing my blond wispy hair every which way. The air rushes inside of my chest, puffing me up like a big balloon.

"Look at me, Dad. I am your little love balloon!" I shriek with glee. He laughs. This is a magical experience that I never want to end. This specific moment in time will stay with me forever. I will play it over and over again.

My dad lifts me up higher in the sky. I stretch my hand out, wanting to touch the cotton clouds—to put some magic inside my pocket. Yes, this is a day to remember; my daddy is playing with me again! My feet gently touch the pavement again. The people all around tower over me. The world towers over me. I hide next to my dad's thighs and smile, suddenly feeling a little shy.

We head down the path to our local shops. I know where we are headed; my dad wouldn't forget. He would buy me a small gift after a hard day's work. Like clockwork, we would recreate this moment, our little game, once a week like this. The door bell to one particular shop rings as we push through. "Go on, princess," my dad says. "Have a look!" He wanted my childhood to stay safe in his hands. He wanted to protect me instead of forcing me to rush ahead of my years. He would buy toys that were too big for me, knowing he didn't have much time with me anymore. Behind the big double-glass doors stood doll carriages, bikes, and talking dolls. They were all waiting for me to catch up with them. My dad was older than he felt inside, and he tried not to let that get in the way of our father-daughter time. Even so, all those lovely toys gleamed as new. Little did he know that they would never be played with by me.

The toys were bought in love for the childhood I would never have. But that was okay. Things do not always turn out as we plan because the world has bigger plans for all of us. But this particular moment stands still. I see and remember the toys at home, waiting for me. "Princess, look at this . . ." my dad says with a smile. He hopes I will love it. I smile back. He doesn't know that the biggest gift money can't buy was standing there in front of me—him.

"Dad, it didn't matter that I never got a chance to play with toys like other children do," I reassure him. "I had something better. I had and still have the gift of love I share inside with you. It can't get broken. A wheel can't fall off. This gift is all mine and it stays intact. We both have a key inside our hearts to open the treasure chest of whatever we want to play. That's all I ever needed."

It feels like a day that will never end, and I don't want it to. We have a magic that lasts forever in a world that never closes or sleeps. I meet him after a hard day's work. I am his princess; yes, that's me. I nod my head in delight and enjoy my rushed childhood with my dad.

He gently rests the tea set on the counter at the front of the shop. He calls us "regulars" at the shop and the word makes me smile. My dad pays for the gifts and the shopkeeper tells us to have a lovely day. We know we will. My dad grabs a hold of my small hand and gently squeezes it. I skip along next to his great big strides, trying to keep up with his long strides. I'm still giggling; it's like I can't stop when we're together. He opens the front door to our house and Mom calls out from the kitchen. "Dinner is on and won't be long!" she says. We rush in to the dining room like two little kids. I climb up on my dad's knee and look at him. I already know what he's going to ask. "So, princess, shall we make some tea?"

I nod and we pretend to drink from our pretty cups. We even make sipping sounds and sighs to show how much we enjoy our make believe tea. After tea and dinner, my dad opens the big glass doors and reaches for the walking and talking doll. He still wants to play with me! He lifts the doll from out of its box and turns a crank in its back. Suddenly, it's talking and walking toward me. I scream and run away, hiding behind my dad's big chair. I don't understand how a make believe doll can speak and walk like a human. I'm afraid of what I don't understand. My dad puts the doll back in its box and, thankfully, I never see it again.

What a mixture of adventures we would have—adventures, at times, too old for me. I saw things a child should not see. But the love inside made me feel safe anyway, regardless of whatever kind of experiences we had.

. . . I see myself rushing through the corridors with my half brother to find my dad. He is twenty nine years older than me; his hands are big like my dad's. He peers into multiple windows of various closed doors. I try my best to simply keep up with him.

"Ah! This is it!" he finally says, coming to an abrupt halt.

"Let me see!" I beg, pulling at his trousers around his knee. I miss my dad. I don't understand what's wrong .

He slowly pushes the door open. There isn't just one bed, but rows of many. Where are we? *I wonder.* This place sure smells funny! *I scan the beds and finally spot my dad in his bed at the end of the row. Funny-looking curtains hang on poles around each bed. "Dad!" I cry out at the top of my lungs.*

"Shhh!" my half brother shushes me. "Don't make so much noise in here! Keep quiet. People are asleep. Please try to keep quiet as you speak, okay?"

I nod and immediately try to make the soles of my shoes silent as they squelch with the rubber and make contact with the floor. We approach my dad and I take hold of the blanket that is hanging off one side of the bed. I want to get my dad's attention but I don't know how.

My half brother gives me a slightly irritated look. "Don't annoy Dad," he whispers. He looks at my dad and shrugs. My dad smiles and asks my half brother to lift me up onto his big bed. I give him a hug and wait for him to speak.

"Hello, my princess," he says weakly. His voice is fragile, but he still has a twinkle in his eyes. Somehow I know that something is wrong though. I begin to get nervous. His breathing seems shallow and he's quiet—too quiet.

"Can we play today?" I ask him hopefully, ignoring the eye rolling of my half brother next to me.

"No, Dad is tired today," my half brother speaks up when my dad doesn't answer right away.

My dad clears his throat and now offers small talk in a tone more serious than I have ever known. Still, he smiles reassuringly and takes my hand. His hold silences my thoughts. The silence now fills around the bed. I don't mind the eerie quietness though for this is my dad. This is what he wants. My heart glows with love for him. "I love you, Dad," I whisper, unsure of what else I should say in this moment. "I will see you soon . . ."

"We will, princess," he silently replies with a nod. As my half brother and I leave the room of many beds, I turn my head back to smile one more time. His hand had fallen off the side of the bed—a little movement. Was he waving goodbye to me? I envision his hand and begin thinking about all the times he had held mine, making me feel safe. It would become a memory I would never forget. I think about my dad as we walk back through the corridors and the many doors to the parking garage. Our last conversation plays over and over in my mind.

"I love you, Dad. I will see you soon . . ."

"We will, princess."

My half brother and I never did get the chance to say goodbye. But looking back, I now know why. The truth is that my dad never really left me; he didn't really *die*. We still meet up in the shades of the night. We meet half way to the magic room we created. We continue our game where we last left off. We experience a continuation of life, hand in hand.

Even though my dad has gone to the other side of the fence, we often communicate with each other. He helps me work things out in my mind. He helps me remember the good experiences I had with him and my mother, and he reminds me that I am not alone.

I remember, Dad. Can you see? I remember how much I love you and you love me. It is still fresh like the glistening of a new toy, not discarded or broken in bits. We have nothing we ever will need to fix . . .

I will meet you at the bottom of our path on the grass land outside our gate. We will have more fun when you finish work. What game should we play next? Dad, I cried every second of the day after you went to the afterlife. During those sad times, I only saw darkness around me. I was numb to my bones—cloaked in a blanket of death, a place that has taken me years to understand. But with each new chapter of my life, the warm rays of our love soon melted the frozen snow. I could see you once again. My dark tears of loss and confusion numbed any feeling left inside me, but you helped me realize the truth.

At times, I was out of my own depth in a world full of strangers who didn't understand me. You were the only one who saw a princess in me. Others saw my tears. They saw the ugly mess of my childhood's history. But your spirit helped remind me that I was and always will be me under all the hard rock I had built up to protect myself. My tears no longer fall. I have changed into a bright new dress full of color like the rainbows in the sky. I now see cotton clouds floating by. I can dream again.

"Welcome home, Princess," I hear you say. "What a long day today has been."

I smile, seeing him, and open the front door of our room in our hearts. I hold his hand tight once again and share each chapter all the same—our story from both sides of the fence. It is a continuation of what we know, a life always beginning with no end. Our father-daughter love will never break; it is too strong.

"I love you, Dad," I say back. There are no other words I need to speak in this moment.

I have grown since we last met, don't you think? *I'm a big girl now. I mean, Look at my legs! In this moment, I hold my arms outstretched far and wide with a twinkle in my eye and grin, poised for a hug.* You know what's coming, don't you, Dad? I love you so much.

My mind continues with the images, the experiences, the memories. Suddenly, I hear feet around my head. My eyes flutter open to see a very small room. In the far corner of the room, I see a tiny glistening sliver of light. What is the light? *I wonder. I try to move my arms but they are placed down by my sides.* What!? *This room is not a room after all.* Where am I? Where is this?

I strain my eyes to see from the slit in the corner of this confined space. I can make out bright green grass and people's feet—some sneakers are white, some black. I listen carefully and hear giggling; people are playing catch. Why can I only see people's feet? *I touch around me and feel wood. I am in a box of some kind.* But why am I in a box? What is going on? *To my relief, the lid is not locked or closed up tight. I can still see daylight. People are holding hands and having so much fun. Still, my rear end is beginning to get numb; I must get out. I try to feel for the lid of this box, but I can't seem to reach it. I call out, "Please, someone, help me get out of here!"*

No one hears my little voice inside this box. I am buried underneath the grass that others are playing on. Oddly, no one notices me even *though I still see them, even if all I can see are their feet. I pull at the lid once more. It is broken. Beginning to panic, I claw at the earth with my fingernails and try to pound it with my fists. The earth falls inside the wooden box with me. Now I am more than confused.* Am I dead? No, I am not. I know that I'm not. *I desperately want to join the others in the games that they're playing. I want to participate in a game of ball or hide-and-seek. (Even though I'm already hidden so well that no one can see me . . .)*

I garner my mental and physical strength and use all of my will power to climb out of the grave—a box for the flesh and bones, my vehicle, that has served me so well. Looking down, I see that I have a new dress on, and a new body—one that my dad will recognize when we play our games again. It is a body that will never outgrow me; it had waited patiently for me to remember the truth year after year. My experiences filled up chapters of laughter and despair; this is my book, one that illustrates a true life well-lived. I have no regrets.

Fresh air fills me up. I see the grass, so lovely and green, and all the flowers blowing in the breeze. I see dogs barking and children giggling in delight. My welcome home is a breathtaking sight to behold . . .

What a wonderful world in which we live—one world with a great big fence that separates two sides that are so different yet the same. It is a world full of excitement if only we open our eyes. We should stand on the tips of our toes to look over the fence and enjoy the view. The other side of the fence, the afterlife, is our true home. It's a place that welcomes us home for all eternity. Remember, life is a continuation and we all hold the key to eternal happiness. Guard yours close.

RIP stands for *remembers in peace*. One day, we will all remember a life of magic that never ends. You'll see.